Building English Skills

**Blue Level
Canadian Edition**

Skills Practice Book

Skills Practice Books

Purple Level

Yellow Level

BLUE LEVEL

Orange Level

Green Level

Red Level

Gold Level

Silver Level

Aqua Level

Brown Level

 IRWIN PUBLISHING
Toronto, Canada

Special Features of This Skills Practice Book

- It contains thousands of skill-building exercises in composition, vocabulary, grammar, usage, capitalization, punctuation, spelling, and good manuscript form.

- Each page is a self-contained unit. It contains a brief explanation, followed by an average of twenty reinforcing exercises.

- Each page focuses on one—and only one—topic or skill.

- Key words and phrases are printed in color for greater clarity and ease of use.

- A comprehensive review lesson follows each major section of the text.

This Canadian edition, prepared by the Staff of Irwin Publishing, is derived from the Skills Practice Book conceived and developed by the Staff of McDougal, Littell & Company.

Joy Littell, Editorial Director
Kathleen Laya, Managing Editor
Elizabeth M. Garber, Assistant Editor

Specific materials for this book were prepared by the following:

John Glavin, Chairperson, English Department
 Glenbrook North High School, Northbrook, Illinois
Nancy Kellman, teacher and writer
Kathleen Minard, teacher and writer

Canadian Cataloguing in Publication Data
 Main entry under title:
 Skills practice book, blue level

 (Building English skills)
 For use in grade 10.
 ISBN 0-7725-5142-1

 1. English language—Composition and exercises.
 I. Series.

 LB1576.S67   428.2   C82-095240-0

Paragraph on page 25 adapted, with kind permission, from the pamphlet *Visit Famous Casa Loma* operated by the Kiwanis Club of West Toronto, 1 Austin Terrace, Toronto, Ontario M5R 1X8; Review listing on page 49 from the *Journal of Canadian Fiction* Number 23, 1979, page 202

ISBN 0-7725-5142-1 (Student's)   ISBN 0-7725-5143-X (Teacher's)

Copyright © 1982 by McDougal, Littell & Company
This edition Copyright © 1983, Irwin Publishing
6 7 8 9 MP 04 03 02 01
Printed and bound in Canada

Contents

Composition

Contents

Grammar and Usage

Composition

Prefixes

A **prefix** is a syllable, or group of syllables, placed in front of a root to change the meaning of the root. For example:

mis-	+	interpret	=	misinterpret
re-	+	locate	=	relocate
dis-	+	connect	=	disconnect

The following prefixes are useful to know because each has a single meaning:

PREFIXES HAVING A SINGLE MEANING

bene-	=	good		**intro-**	=	into
circum-	=	around		**mal-**	=	bad
equi-	=	equal		**mis-**	=	wrong
extra-	=	outside		**non-**	=	not
intra-	=	within		**pre-**	=	before

There are some prefixes that are useful in unlocking word meanings even though they have more than one meaning.

PREFIXES HAVING MORE THAN ONE MEANING

dis-	=	opposite of	**sub-**	=	under
	=	depriving of		=	below
	=	away		=	at the bottom
in- (ir-, il-, im-)	=	not	**pro-**	=	in favor of
	=	in		=	before
	=	very		=	forward
super-	=	over and above	**trans-**	=	across
	=	beyond		=	beyond
re-	=	again	**un-**	=	not
	=	back		=	the opposite of

Determining the Meaning of Prefixes. Break each of the following words into word parts. Give the meaning of the prefix and the whole word. Consult a dictionary if necessary.

Example: superannuated *over and above in age or years*

1. equidistant _____
2. circumnavigate _____
3. illegal _____
4. misinform _____
5. repossess _____
6. presuppose _____
7. malfunction _____
8. disassociate _____
9. subterranean _____
10. transport _____

Suffixes (I)

A **suffix** is a syllable, or group of syllables, placed after a root to form a new word.

ROOT		SUFFIX		NEW WORD
scholar	+	ship	=	scholarship
manage	+	ment	=	management
sad	+	ness	=	sadness

Noun Suffixes. The following groups of noun suffixes can help you increase your ability to recognize the basic meaning of words.

NOUN SUFFIXES THAT MEAN "ONE WHO DOES SOMETHING"

-eer	electioneer	**-ist**	typist
-er	stenographer	**-ician**	physician

NOUN SUFFIXES THAT MAKE ABSTRACT WORDS

-ance, -ence	reluctance, dependence	**-ment**	improvement
-ation, -tion	determination, correction	**-ness**	shyness
-dom	freedom	**-ship**	authorship
-hood	childhood	**-tude**	solitude
-ice	cowardice	**-ty, -ity**	loyalty, equality
-ism	socialism		

Determining the Meaning of Suffixes. Break each of the following words into word parts. Give the meaning of the suffix and the whole word. Use a dictionary if necessary.

1. nationalism _____
2. embarrassment _____
3. stillness _____
4. engineer _____
5. physicist _____
6. celebration _____
7. possibility _____
8. justice _____
9. clinician _____
10. novelty _____

Using Noun Suffixes. Add a noun suffix to each of the words below. Watch for spelling changes.

1. ideal _____   5. legal _____
2. type _____   6. commune _____
3. lazy _____   7. magic _____
4. special _____   8. note _____

Suffixes (II)

Adjective Suffixes. The following groups of adjective suffixes will help you increase your ability to recognize the basic meanings of words.

ADJECTIVE SUFFIXES THAT MEAN "FULL OF"

-ous	curious	**-acious**	vivacious
-ose	verbose	**-ful**	painful

ADJECTIVE SUFFIXES THAT MEAN "RELATING TO" OR "PERTAINING TO"

-al	lyrical	**-ish**	fiendish
-ic	comic	**-ive, -ative**	objective, talkative
-ical	economical		

ADJECTIVE SUFFIXES THAT MEAN WHAT THEY SAY

-able, -ible	readable, edible	**-less**	tasteless
-most	topmost	**-like**	childlike

Determining the Meaning of Suffixes. Break the following words into word parts. Give the meaning of the suffix and the whole word. Consult a dictionary if necessary.

1. glorious _____
2. grandiose _____
3. structural _____
4. restful _____
5. original _____
6. historic _____
7. theatrical _____
8. dangerous _____
9. childish _____
10. creative _____
11. convertible _____
12. uppermost _____
13. visible _____
14. timeless _____
15. lifelike _____

Using Adjective Suffixes. Add an adjective suffix to each of the words below.

1. beauty _____	4. peril _____
2. defect _____	5. mystery _____
3. valor _____	6. architecture _____

Roots

The **root** is the part of a word that contains the basic meaning. Each of the following Latin roots is responsible for a whole family of English words. If you know the meanings of these roots, you will be able to determine the basic meaning of many new words.

SIXTEEN USEFUL LATIN ROOTS

capt	=	take, hold, seize	capture, captive
cede, cess	=	yield, give away	concede, concession
cred	=	believe	credible, credo
dic, dict	=	speak, say	dictaphone, dictator
duc, duct	=	lead	conduct, induction
fac, fec	=	do, make	manufacture, defect
mit, miss	=	send	admit, dismiss
pon, pos, posit	=	place, put	postpone, deposit
port	=	carry	import, deport
scrib, script	=	write	transcribe, inscription
spec	=	look	inspect, spectacles
stat	=	stand, put in place	statue, status
vers, vert	=	turn	reverse, convert
vid, vis	=	see	visible, video
voc, vok	=	call	vocalize, invoke
vol	=	wish	malevolent, volunteer

Determining Meaning by Using Latin Roots. Define each of the following words. Use a dictionary if necessary.

1. captive _____

2. access _____

3. credibility _____

4. prediction _____

5. deduction _____

6. facility _____

7. remission _____

8. subversive _____

9. transmit _____

10. portable _____

11. scribble _____

12. spectacle _____

13. stationary _____

14. position _____

15. visor _____

16. revert _____

17. revoke _____

Word Families

A word family is a group of words that have a common root. As you have learned, the Latin root *voc* or *vok* means "call." Many English words contain this root: *vocal, vocalize, evoke, vocation.*

Many additional words that contain this root have prefixes added in front of the word: pro*voke*, re*voke*, in*voke*.

Still other words that contain this root have both prefixes and suffixes: in*voca*tion, sub*voca*lize, pro*voca*tion.

Being able to identify the root in a longer word will help you unlock its meaning. Also, seeing how words are grouped into word families will give you a method of sorting out the many words you will meet in your reading and use in your speech.

Working with Word Families. Identify the root in each group of words below. Give its basic meaning. Be sure you can define each of the words in the "family."

1. prescribe, describe, scripture, inscription, postscript

   _____

2. credit, incredible, discredit, credibility, credence

   _____

3. vision, televise, revise, visible, visit

   _____

4. station, statue, status, stationary (adjective), thermostat

   _____

5. dictate, prediction, benediction, dictaphone, malediction

   _____

Identifying Word Families. Under each word below, write as many words as you can think of that contain the same root. Begin by underlining the root.

1. portable   2. respect   3. admit

   _____   _____   _____

   _____   _____   _____

   _____   _____

   _____   _____

Review: Building Your Vocabulary   6

Determining Meaning from Word Parts. Define each of the words below by analyzing prefixes, suffixes, and Latin roots. Define the separate word parts and the whole word. Consult a dictionary if necessary.

Example: invisible _not capable of being seen_

1. revert _return to a former habit._
2. captive _held prisoner_
3. proposition _plan suggested for acceptance_
4. deport _to expel from a country_
5. benediction _an utterance of good wishes_
6. involuntary _against ones will_
7. remittance _the sending of money_
8. prescription _a written order_
9. transmission _the act of process_
10. produce _to bring forth_

Using Prefixes and Suffixes To Alter Word Meanings. Add the prefix or suffix required to change the meaning of the given word as indicated in parentheses.

Example: legible (not) _illegible_

1. photographs (one who does) _photographer_
2. depend (the state of being) _dependincy_
3. distant (equal) _equidistant_
4. responsible (not) _irrisponsible_
5. stress (full of) _stressful_
6. convert (capable of being) _converting_
7. history (relating to) _historical_
8. standard (below) _substandard_
9. auction (one who) _auctioneer_
10. mystery (full of) _mysterious_

What's in a Dictionary Entry?

The dictionary is an invaluable aid to every educated person; unfortunately, many people do not know how to get the most out of a dictionary entry for a word. Study this entry.

lo·qua·cious (lo kwa′shəs) *adj.* [< L. *loquax* < *loqui*, to speak] very talkative; fond of talking —see **SYN.** at TALKATIVE —lo-qua′cious·ly adv. —lo-qua′cious·ness n.

Entry Word. Printed in dark type, the entry word is divided into syllables.

Pronunciation. Following the entry word, the pronunciation is given in parentheses. By using the pronunciation key at the bottom of the dictionary page, you can determine the pronunciation.

Parts of Speech. The abbreviation *adj.* following the pronunciation indicates that *loquacious* is an adjective.

Etymology. The material printed within the dark brackets gives the etymology or origin of the word. Here, *loquacious* comes from a Latin word meaning "to speak."

Definition. Following the etymology, you find the definition or definitions of the word.

Synonymy. The abbreviation SYN. indicates a *synonymy*, which is a discussion of words that have similar meanings.

Derived Words. The additional words, *loquaciously* and *loquaciousness*, printed in bold type and divided into syllables, are words that are derived from *loquacious*. They are so closely related to the entry word that they are not listed separately.

Using Dictionary Entries. Find the following information in any good dictionary. Put the name of the dictionary you are using on the blank below.

www.dictionary.com

1. Copy the pronunciation of *jurisprudence*.

   [joor-is-prood-ns]

2. What is the etymology of the word *mutton*?

   Middle English

3. What is the definition of *predatory*?

   preying on other organisms.

4. What is a synonym for *aphorism*?

   Saying

5. What is the difference in meaning between *suggest* and *insinuate*?

   suggest-to mention or introduce
   insinuate-to suggest or hint.

Multiple Meanings of Words

Many of the words listed in the dictionary have more than one meaning. A good way to develop your vocabulary is to learn additional meanings for words that are already part of your vocabulary.

Working with Multiple Meanings. The word *rake* is used in many different ways in the sentences below. On the blank after each sentence, define the word *rake* as it is used in that particular sentence. Consult a dictionary when necessary.

1. We used the *rake* for gathering the leaves.

   a tool to rake leaves

2. We will really *rake* in the money with our new business venture.

   to gather or collect

3. The reporter *raked* up facts that had been hushed up for years.

   to gather or collect

4. Carefully, the campers *raked* the fire before they moved on.

   to clear

5. The troopers will *rake* the countryside looking for the lost child.

   to search throughly

Writing Sentences with Words Having Multiple Meanings. The word *fine* has many different meanings. Consult a dictionary and locate five meanings for the word. Write a sentence for each of the separate meanings. Each sentence should clearly illustrate the meaning of the word.

1. _That was a really fine wine._
2. _The sand was very fine._
3. _The knife is fine enough to carve well._
4. _He is a very fine musician._
5. _It's a fine day today._

Finding Multiple Meanings in the Dictionary. Look through the dictionary and locate two words with multiple meanings. Write the words and at least three of their meanings below.

Word 1 _For_   Word 2 _Still_

1. _purpose of._   1. _remaining in place_
2. _intended to belong to_   2. _free from sound_
3. _in order to obtain_   3. _subdued_

Synonyms

You can help refine or sharpen your vocabulary through the correct use of **synonyms.** Synonyms are words that have similar meanings. There are, however, various shades of meaning to words similar enough to be considered synonyms.

Determining Shades of Meaning Among Synonyms. Each of the following words shares the general meaning of "a person in opposition to another," yet each word has a more exact meaning. Give a specific definition of each.

1. enemy _One who feels hatred toward another_
2. opponent _a person who is on an opposing side_
3. competitor _one that competes with another._
4. rival _one who attempts to equal_
5. foe _a personal enemy_

Using Synonyms. For each word below, list three synonyms. Use each synonym in a sentence illustrating the exact meaning of the word.

accident   1. _collision_   2. _disaster_   3. _Fluke_
1. _I was in a big collision._
2. _There was a big disaster._
3. _"What a big fluke!"_

think   1. _assume_   2. _resolve_   3. _ponder_
1. _I assume it would be create_
2. _I'm resolving the question._
3. _He pondered his next words thoroughly_

warm   1. _toast_   2. _heat_   3. _thaw_
1. _The house was warm and toasty_
2. _The fireplace heated the house_
3. _I let the fish thaw out._

quiet   1. _noiseless_   2. _speechless_   3. _peaceful_
1. _The room was noiseless_
2. _She was speechless._
3. _It was nice and peaceful now._

leader   1. _captain_   2. _manager_   3. _General_
1. _He was the captain of the team._
2. _John Ferguson is the manager of the Maple Leafs._
3. _I saw the commander of the boat._

Review: Using the Dictionary

Obtaining Information from Dictionary Entries. Use a dictionary to answer the following questions.

1. What part of speech is *impute*? <u>verb</u>

2. What are the various meanings of the word *liable*? _____
   - legally responsible
   - susceptible

3. What is the pronunciation of *clandestine*? On which syllable does the accent fall? [klan-des-tin] The accent falls on "des"

4. What are three synonyms for the word *mirth*? Use each in a sentence.
   Fun - I had so much fun
   Glee - He shouted with glee
   Happiness - The room was filled with happiness.

5. What is the etymology of the word *phobia*? 1780-90
   Greek "phobos" = fear.

Working with Multiple Meanings. The word *stand* has many meanings. Find at least five different meanings for the word. Write a sentence for each illustrating the *specific* meaning of the word as used.

1. I am standing up.
2. She stands six feet tall.
3. He stands for free trade
4. The building stands on Rebbecca and Dundas St.
5. The ruins still stand.

Working with Synonyms. Each of the following words shares the general meaning of "to disapprove." Some, however, are much more serious in meaning than others. Use each in a sentence, illustrating the specific meaning of the word. Then, on the blank before each number, rank each word from 1 to 4: **1,** most severe; **4,** least severe. Use a dictionary.

2 1. rebuke To express sharp dissapproval
3 2. chide to express dissaproval
4 3. admonish to caution against something
1 4. condemn to express strong dissaproval

Avoiding Empty Sentences   11

Sentences that say too little are **empty sentences.** Grammatically they may be complete; yet, they are lacking in ideas, in substance. They may contain words that repeat an idea contained earlier in the sentence. Sentences are empty because the writer does not think ahead about what he or she wants to say. The reader then gets the impression that the writer is just trying to fill up space.

In order to improve empty sentences, you may have to add facts or ideas.

> EMPTY   I was unhappy at summer camp because I didn't like it there.
>
> IMPROVED   I was unhappy at summer camp because I was lonely and bored.

Another way to improve an empty sentence is to shorten it.

> EMPTY   He won the trophy for best player because he was the best player on the team.
>
> IMPROVED   He won the trophy because he was the best player on the team.

Revising Empty Sentences. Rewrite the following empty sentences.

1. Our basketball team won the game by scoring more baskets than our opponents scored.

Our team ~~one~~ won the game by scoring more baskets.

2. The roads are more crowded at rush hour because there are more cars on them during that busy period.

The roads are more crowded because there are more cars.

3. I didn't make it to class on time because I was late.

I didn't make it to class on time because I didn't get to school on time.

4. Medicine has made little progress against degenerative diseases that gradually get worse.

Medicine has made little progress against diseases that get worse.

5. Having finished the test, I checked the questions I had finished to see if I had finished everything.

Having finished the test, I checked to see if I did everything.

6. Weekly news magazines, if you read them every week, are a good way of keeping up with the news that happened during the week.

Weekly news magazines are a good way to see what happened during the week.

7. I don't type well, and I don't have good handwriting, either, but my typing is really not good.

I struggle at typing and handwriting.

8. The roads were impassable because of the rain, and no one could get through.

The roads were ~~good~~ jammed because of the rain.

Avoiding Padded Sentences   12

Padded sentences are sentences that are stretched out with unnecessary words. Such sentences are ineffective and lacking in force.

Padding can result from the following:

repetition of the same word or idea
repetition of *that*
use of fillers such as "on account of . . .", "the reason is that . . .",
   "what I believe is . . .", "the thing . . ."

To revise padded sentences, omit the padding.

PADDED   What I think is that we need a new car.
BETTER   I think we need a new car.

Revising Padded Sentences. Revise the following sentences.

1. Today, many modern cities are more advanced than those of yesterday.

   Many Modern cities are more advanced

2. In my opinion, I think bicycling is the best exercise in the world.

   I think bicycling is the best exercise.

3. I don't know for sure, and I may be wrong, but I think I saw Ellen in the cafeteria with Jim.

   I think I saw Ellen in the cafeteria with Jim

4. On account of the fact that it rained, our picnic plans were cancelled.

   Our picnic plans were cancelled.

5. It is important that since they don't like pizza that we don't serve it.

   Since they don't like pizza, we won't serve it.

6. The reason I didn't get a ten-speed bike was that I couldn't afford it.

   I didn't get at ten-speed bike because I couldn't afford it.

7. When we had our garage sale, it was on account of the fact that we had too much junk in the garage.

   We had to much junk at our garage sale.

8. The thing I am concerned about most is the ecology.

   I am concerned about ecology.

9. I was told that if I didn't pass English that I would have to go to summer school.

   If I didn't pass english, I would go to summer school.

10. What I don't like about French fries is when French fries are greasy.

   I don't like French Fries when there greasy

Avoiding Overloaded Sentences   13

Overloaded sentences are sentences that say too much. They carry too many ideas. They mix up important ideas with unimportant ones. In order to avoid overloaded sentences, you should

1. First, decide on the main ideas.
2. Decide which ideas can be combined into one sentence.
3. Write the main ideas as one sentence, following the usual sentence pattern of subject—verb—object.
4. Write separate sentences for the other ideas.
5. Write simply and clearly.

OVERLOADED   I would like to enrol in Business Administration, but I know that my mathematics marks shall have to improve.

REVISED   I would like to enrol in Business Administration. I know, however, that my mathematics marks shall have to improve.

Revising Overloaded Sentences. Revise each of the following sentences.

1. While he took care of the baby, the babysitter was earning $2.65 an hour, and he needed the money to buy a guitar.

While he took care of the baby, he was earning $2.65 an hour. He needs the money to buy his guitar.

2. In English class we are studying grammar now and last semester I eventually learned how to diagram a sentence, which is very difficult to learn.

In English class we are studying grammar. Last semester I eventually learned how to diagram a sentence. That is very difficult to learn.

3. We are going to Ottawa for vacation and will also visit our grandparents in Montreal, which is an historic old city that we learned about in seventh grade.

We are going to Ottawa for vacation. We will also visit our grandparents in Montreal. It is an historic city that we learned in Grade 7.

4. Mom works all day as a key-punch operator, and our neighbor really wishes she had as good a job as Mom does.

Mom works all day as a key-punch operator. Our neighbor really wishes she had as good a job as Mom does.

5. There was a heavy downpour, and we were worried about our basement flooding, and we hope to carpet the recreation room next year.

There was a heavy downpour. We were worried about our basement flooding. We hope to carpet the rec. room next year.

Keeping to the Point   14

Omit details that interrupt the meaning of a sentence and have no connection with the main idea.

IRRELEVANT DETAILS   Our math teacher, who is the youngest of five children in her family, gave us a long homework assignment.

IMPROVED   Our math teacher gave us a long homework assignment.

Keeping to the Point. Revise the following sentences.

1. The library book that I am reading, which I thought I lost one day, is a biography of Helen Keller.

   The library book that I'm reading is a bio of Helen Keller.

2. From my grandmother I inherited several antique plates collected on her travels around the world, although I have never been around the world myself.

   From my grandmother I inherited several antique plates collected on her travels around the world.

3. Arthur Rubinstein is a virtuoso pianist who seems like a refined person and who fills concert halls.

   Arthur Rubinstein is a virtuoso pianist.

4. The candidate, who resembles my Uncle Bill, spoke knowledgeably about important issues of the campaign.

   The candidate spoke knowledgeably about important issues of the campaign.

5. Mom and Dad made a delicious meal for our guest, who had gone to the beauty shop before our party.

   Mom and Dad made a delicious meal for our guest.

6. Our car, which has denim upholstery, was damaged by a hit-and-run driver.

   Our car was damaged by a hit-and-run driver.

7. Dad was upset about how high our telephone bill was, since it contained several long-distance calls, and I had charged a pair of shoes without asking him.

   Dad was upset about how high our telephone bill was, since it contained several long-distant calls.

8. Mr. Smith, who is a redhead, ushered the clients into his boss's office.

   Mr. Smith ushered the clients into the boss's office.

Combining Related Ideas   **15**

Overuse of simple sentences can make writing choppy and monotonous. You can correct choppy style by combining related ideas into one sentence.

The following are some ways to combine related ideas into compound sentences:

1. Use a conjunction to join the clauses.

   Lee and I wanted to go out for lunch. We didn't have any money.
   Lee and I wanted to go out for lunch, but we didn't have any money.

2. Use a semicolon between the clauses.

   This has been a good summer. I have enjoyed myself.
   This has been a good summer; I have enjoyed myself.

3. Use conjunctive adverbs and other linking words to combine related ideas.

   I like ice cream. I am not supposed to eat foods high in butterfat.
   I like ice cream; however, I am not supposed to eat foods high in butterfat.

Conjunctive adverbs are used after a semicolon and are followed by a comma. Here are some common conjunctive adverbs:

RESULT	ADDITION	
consequently	also	in fact
hence	besides	likewise
therefore	furthermore	moreover
thus	indeed	

ALTERNATIVE	EXCEPTION OR CONTRAST	
at the same time	however	yet
on the other hand	nevertheless	still
otherwise	nonetheless	

Combining Related Ideas. Supply a conjunctive adverb that makes clear the relationship between the parts.

1. I am going to summer school to take typing; _therefore_, I should be able to work part time in the office next fall.

2. The train was scheduled to arrive at 6:30; _yet_, it had not arrived by 7:00.

3. Sarah wants to work at a summer camp; _in fact_, she has already applied for a position.

Combine each simple sentence pair into one effective compound sentence.

1. The freezer was broken. The ice was melting.
   The freezer was broken; therefore, the ice was melting

2. The team captain was thrown out of the game. We won anyway.
   The team captain was thrown out of the game; nonetheless, we won anyway.

3. The picnic is scheduled for Saturday. It is supposed to rain.
   The picnic is scheduled for Saturday; on the other hand, it is supposed to rain.

Keeping Related Parts Together   16

Keep sentence parts which are related in thought close together in construction.

AWKWARD   I am, when I finish eating this ice cream, going for a bike ride.
    (Parts of the verb are separated.)

BETTER   When I finish eating this ice cream, I am going for a bike ride.

AWKWARD   Debbie, after getting her ears pierced, was excited about buying
    her first earrings. (Subject and verb are separated.)

BETTER   After getting her ears pierced, Debbie was excited about buying
    her first earrings.

AWKWARD   I bought, when I was downtown, new gym shoes.
    (Verb and object are separated.)

BETTER   I bought new gym shoes when I was downtown.

Keeping Related Parts Together. Revise each sentence below by keeping related parts together.

1. Our car was, while parked on the street, sideswiped.

   While parked on the street, our car was sideswiped.

2. I was reading, while relaxing on the sofa, a new book by Farley Mowat.

   I was reading a new book by Farley Mowat, while relaxing on the sofa.

3. Julie, while drinking a glass of iced tea, finished her homework.

   Julie finished her homework, while drinking a glass of iced tea.

4. Dad is, whenever someone leaves a bike in the driveway, really annoyed.

   Dad is really annoyed, whenever someone leaves a bike in the driveway.

5. I watched, a few weeks ago, a Hallmark Special on television.

   I watched a Hallmark Special on t.v. a few weeks ago.

6. Joey is having, now that he is in fourth grade, difficulty with his classwork.

   Now that he is in fourth, Joey is having difficulty with his classwork.

7. Bob, while playing his electric guitar, was keeping the whole family awake.

   Bob was keeping the whole family awake, while playing his guitar.

8. There are, according to the rules of baseball, nine players on a team.

   According to the rules of baseball, there are nine players on a team

Combining Ideas Effectively

Although *and* is a useful conjunction for joining ideas that are related, its over-use creates a decidedly uninteresting style. Avoid stringing a series of ideas together with *and's*.

Compound sentences are valuable because they tell the reader that two ideas are related. Sometimes a writer joins unrelated ideas. This confuses the reader. Sometimes, the writer has not taken time to plan and has left out ideas that are needed to explain how the two sentences are related. Sometimes the ideas would be better written in two separate sentences.

Combining Ideas Effectively. Follow these suggestions as you revise the sentences below.

1. Check the sentence for too many *and's*.
2. Pick out the main idea.
3. Combine related ideas.
4. Separate the compound sentences that join unrelated ideas.
5. Supply the details needed to make good sense.
6. Write more than one sentence if necessary.

1. Dad takes vitamins every morning, and he works out at the gym once a week and he is going to see the doctor for a check-up next month.

> Dad takes vitamins every morning, and he is going to see the doctor for a checkup next month. He works out at the gym once a week.

2. I was constantly interrupted as I worked on my composition, and the doorbell rang, and my pen ran out of ink.

> I was constantly interrupted as I worked on my composition. The doorbell rang, and my pen ran out of ink.

3. I came to Canada as a small boy, and my brother came also and I am now a Canadian citizen.

> Me and my brother came to Canada as small boys. I am now a canadian citizen.

4. I took my girlfriend to the movie, and tickets were more expensive than we expected, and we had to walk home.

> I took my girlfriend to the movie, but the tickets were more expensive than we expected, so we had to walk home.

5. My dog has to be taken for walks and he doesn't always want to go, but mother insists.

> My dog has to be taken for walks. He doesn't always want to go, but my mother insists

Subordinating Ideas Correctly 18

Another way to join ideas effectively is to use the complex sentence. The main idea is then expressed in the main clause and the less important idea in the subordinate clause.

SUBORDINATE IDEA   MAIN IDEA

After we had been swimming, we stayed in the shade to avoid sunburn.

Two additional problems in joining ideas are **faulty coordination** and **faulty subordination.**

In **faulty coordination,** the writer joins two ideas that obviously are not of equal value and cannot be joined by *and*. Faulty coordination can be corrected by changing one of the clauses into a subordinate clause, a phrase, or an appositive.

FAULTY   I spent three hours cleaning my room, and Mom said it looked nice.

REVISED   After I spent three hours cleaning my room, Mom said it looked nice.

Faulty subordination occurs when the writer states the main idea in a subordinate clause.

FAULTY   Jerry was reading the newspaper while he kept falling asleep.

REVISED   While he was reading the newspaper, Jerry kept falling asleep.

Coordinating and Subordinating Ideas. Revise the sentences below to correct mistakes in faulty coordination and subordination.

1. Whenever Melinda studies, she has a chemistry test.

   Melinda studies whenever she has a chemistry

2. Because I am putting my allowance in the bank, I have to pay for the window I broke while playing softball.

   I have to put my allowance in the bank because I have to pay for the window that I broke.

3. Grandma got the flu, and we were all away on vacation.

   When we were all on vacation, my grandma got the flu.

4. I fell off my skateboard, and my ankle was broken in two places.

   My ankle was broken in two places when I fell off my skateboard.

5. Our house is getting too small for us, and we saw a real estate agent about trying to sell it.

   Because our house is getting to small for us, we saw a real estat agent about selling it

6. It rained steadily for an hour, and we decided to cancel the parade.

   We decided to cancel the parade because it rained stendily for an hour.

Making Sentence Parts Parallel   19

The coordinating conjunction *and* joins sentence parts of equal value: noun and noun, verb and verb, phrase and phrase, clause and clause. The constructions are then parallel. If *and* is used to join constructions of different kinds, there is a lack of parallelism.

FAULTY   He enjoyed visiting Athens and to see Rome.
        (gerund and infinitive)

REVISED   He enjoyed visiting Athens and seeing Rome.

FAULTY   The doctor told me to take some pills and I shouldn't eat any fruit or vegetables until the rash cleared up.
        (infinitive and clause)

REVISED   The doctor told me to take some pills and not to eat any fruit or vegetables until the rash cleared up.

Lack of parallelism often occurs when the pronouns *which* and *who* are used in a sentence.

FAULTY   John is my neighbor and who has a beautiful flower garden each year. (*and* joins noun and clause.)

REVISED   John is my neighbor, and he has a beautiful flower garden each year.

SIMPLER   John, my neighbor, has a beautiful flower garden each year.

Parallelism. Revise these sentences to make the constructions parallel.

1. I practiced playing the piano and how to read symphonic scores.

   I practiced playing the piano and reading symphonic scores.

2. We listened to the radio and which broadcast an interesting interview.

   We listened to the radio and was broadcasting an interesting interview.

3. The house was large, luxurious, and nice furnishings.

   The large, luxurious house had nice furnishings.

4. The lottery was won by a truck driver and who says he will quit his job now.

   A truck driver won the lottery who says he will quit his job.

5. At camp we learned horseback riding, water skiing, and to pitch a tent.

   We learned horseback riding, water skiing, and pitching a tent all at camp.

6. My sister told me to leave and I shouldn't bother her.

   I shouldn't bother my sister because she told me to leave.

7. My typewriter is old and which needs some repair.

   My old typewriter needs some repair.

8. We planned to shop all afternoon and eating in a nice restaurant.

   We shopped all afternoon and planned eating at a nice restaurant.

Review: Improving Your Sentences 20

Improve the following sentences by

Avoiding empty sentences
Avoiding padded sentences
Avoiding overloaded sentences
Keeping to the point
Combining related ideas

Keeping related sentence parts together
Combining ideas effectively
Subordinating ideas correctly
Making sentence parts parallel

1. It is my opinion that if people can conserve energy, that they should.

In my opinion, people should conserve energy.

2. The overheated car was, while still running, steaming and hissing.

The over heated car was steaming and hissing while still running.

3. The beans we grew are ready to pick. I will pick them now. We will eat them for dinner.

The beans we grew are ready to to pick; there for, we will eat them for dinner.

4. The auto mechanic said we need new shock absorbers, new brakes and to put in a new oil filter.

The auto mechanic said we need new shocks, brakes, and oil filter.

5. The garbage collectors are on strike, and our garbage smells awful.

Our garbage smells awful because the garbage collectors are on strike.

6. I didn't buy the expensive sweater because it cost too much.

I didn't by the sweater because it was too expensive.

7. The reason I went to bed early is that I am planning to get up before dawn on account of I plan to go fishing.

The reason I went to bed early is I am planning to go fishing.

8. There was a terrible pile-up on the highway, and many people were injured, and we were late to the party.

The was a terrible pile up on the highway. Many people were injured, and we were late to the party.

The Definition of a Paragraph

A paragraph is a group of closely related sentences dealing with a single topic or idea. Usually, one sentence, called the **topic sentence,** states the main idea of the paragraph. All the other sentences must be related to this topic sentence. These sentences further explain or support the main idea and give the paragraph a feeling of **unity.**

One problem you may have in regard to writing paragraphs is trying to decide just how long your paragraphs should be. Some textbooks recommend that the paragraph be no less than fifty words and no more than three hundred. It is our recommendation, however, that the paragraph be long enough to develop a single idea without boring your reader. Through practice you will learn to vary the length of your paragraphs in order to communicate your ideas with clarity and interest.

Analyzing Paragraphs. Read the following example of a good paragraph:

When you choose a post-secondary institution to attend, there are many issues to consider. You must consider the type of program you wish to pursue and determine which schools offer the most valuable course of study for your goals. You and your family must discuss the relative costs of various types of programs, deciding which schools are affordable to you. Your academic ability must be considered in terms of competition and grade requirements. Your personality must be taken into consideration as well; do you prefer large classes or small, do you like to be with both boys and girls, do you function best in a structured or a loose setting? Choosing a post-secondary institution is a serious endeavour, encompassing many different elements regarding the school, your goals, your abilities, and your preferences.

1. What is the main idea of this paragraph?

   Choosing a post-secondary institution.

2. Which sentence states the main idea?

   When you choose a post-secondary institution to attend, there are many issues to consider.

3. What do sentences two, three, four, and five add to the main idea?

   It tells you what the requirements are to choose a post-secondary school.

4. How does the last sentence relate to the ideas developed in sentences one through five?

   It sums up the information of sentences one through five.

5. In what way is this paragraph unified?

   It has an opening and closing sentence and talks about one topic.

The Topic Sentence (I)

The **topic sentence** states the main idea of the paragraph. It is like a contract between the writer and his or her reader. It promises that the remainder of the paragraph will explain the idea to the reader.

Although the topic sentence may sometimes appear in the middle of a paragraph, and sometimes at the end, its usual position is at the beginning of the paragraph. As such, it performs two tasks:

1. It makes a general statement about what is to follow.
2. It controls and limits what is to be discussed in the remainder of the paragraph.

In the following example, the topic sentence makes a general statement about what is to follow:

> Daddy-longlegs are not spiders, although they are often mistaken for them. They resemble spiders because they have the same number of legs, eight, while insects usually have six. Their eight legs, though, are far longer and thinner than those of a spider. Their bodies are unified and not divided in two as are spider torsos. Even scientists for many years labeled daddy-longlegs incorrectly as spiders. But they are insects called crane flies.

It promises you that the remainder of the paragraph will explain how daddy-longlegs are mistaken for spiders, and how they are different, from spiders.

The topic sentence must be broad enough so that it can be supported or developed by specific detail, through the remainder of the paragraph. For this reason, we say that a topic sentence makes a general statement, or is wider in scope, than the rest of the sentences in the paragraph.

Working with Topic Sentences. Below are four sentence pairs. One sentence in each pair is broad enough to be a good topic sentence. The other is too specific to be developed into a full paragraph. Put a ✔ on the blank before the sentence that would be a good topic sentence.

1. __✔__ Most teenaged drivers are very cautious and mindful of traffic laws.

_____ My neighbor, Mike, got a ticket one week after he got his license.

2. _____ The math achievement test was two hours long.

__✔__ Achievement testing is one way in which school systems assess how well their teachers teach and their students learn.

3. __✔__ Lower back pain is a common ailment of people who sit for long periods of time every day.

_____ My dad has back trouble.

4. __✔__ Many schools offer career education programs, beginning as early as the primary grades.

_____ The career assembly was held this morning during second period in the auditorium.

The Topic Sentence (II)   23

In addition to making a general statement about what is to follow, the topic sentence controls and limits the ideas that can be discussed in the remainder of the paragraph. In its function as a "contract" between writer and reader, it controls what the paragraph contains.

To cover an idea adequately in a paragraph, the topic sentence must be limited or narrowed. If a topic sentence is too broad, it cannot be adequately developed in a paragraph; it would lead to vague generalities, rather than specific details which could develop the idea with clarity.

This topic sentence is too broad to be developed adequately in one paragraph: I like all sports.

A paragraph on this subject would have to deal with a multitude of sports, not allowing the writer to go into detail on why each sport was liked. A better topic sentence would *limit* the ideas by narrowing the subject. For example: I like the pre-game excitement in the baseball stadium. Now, the paragraph can be developed by giving specific details of the experiences encountered in one place, before one game.

Limiting the Topic Sentence. Below, you will find a series of sentence pairs. In each pair, one topic sentence is too general; the other is properly limited in its scope. Place a ✔ on the line before the properly limited topic sentence.

1. _____ Jesse's last practical joke was a real "pain."

   ___✔___ Practical jokes can be dangerous.

2. ___✔___ Raising a child is difficult but rewarding work.

   _____ I know I worry my parents when I don't come home on time.

3. _____ A television program taught me how to save a life.

   ___✔___ Television is a very valuable source of information.

Rewriting Topic Sentences. Following are topic sentences that are too broad. Rewrite each one, limiting its scope.

1. Summer employment can offer a teenager a wealth of experience.

   _____

2. Sports can be dangerous.

   Alot of hockey players got injured because of the physicality.

3. Involvement in school and community activities is enriching.

   _____

4. Children's toys sometimes stifle the imagination.

   _____

Ways of Developing the Paragraph   24

Once you have decided upon—and properly limited—your topic sentence, your next step in writing is to develop the idea in that sentence into a well-organized paragraph. You must now add several more sentences that give additional information. There are several ways of doing this:

1. by using facts or statistics
2. by using specific examples
3. by using an incident or an anecdote
4. by using comparisons or contrasts
5. by giving reasons

Using Facts or Statistics. The most common way to organize a paragraph of **facts or statistics** is to begin with a broad topic sentence. Then, the writer should offer specific facts, concluding with the most important fact. Such a paragraph is organized by moving from the least important facts to the most important facts. This organization allows a writer to build his or her ideas to a climax, or to emphasize a particular point.

Read the following paragraph and notice how the facts are arranged.

> The desert camel has a remarkable energy system that allows it to do without water for days. It uses a type of closed air conditioning by circulation of cycled water. This forestalls sweating until body temperature reaches approximately 41°C. The camel can refrain from drinking water eight days in summer and fifty-six days in winter. At a rare watering hole, it can consume 96.64 litres of water in the record time of ten minutes. Unlike other animals, it loses little water. Instead, it seems to recycle water internally through its lumpy cooling system. The camel must be the envy of its thirsty rider.

The paragraph begins by informing the reader that the camel has a remarkable energy system. The next five sentences give facts about how this energy system operates. The next to the last sentence summarizes the system. The last sentence gives emphasis to the importance of this system, as it contrasts the camel to its thirsty rider.

Developing a Paragraph by Using Facts or Statistics. Choose one of the topics listed below or choose your own topic and develop it into a paragraph using facts or statistics. Do research to obtain information if necessary. Remember to write a topic sentence that controls and limits what is to be discussed.

1. Post-secondary education costs are rising.
2. Some anti-pollution devices waste energy.
3. Ten-speed bicycles are scientifically designed.
4. First aid training is essential for a babysitter.

Using an Example   25

Sometimes the topic sentence will consist of a general truth or general idea that is best supported through the use of a **specific example**. Note how the following paragraph uses a specific example to describe Sir Henry Pellatt's architectural interest in castles.

Sir Henry Pellatt, soldier, financier and industrialist had a life-long interest in castles of medieval times. He used some of his fortune to build Casa Loma. He brought marble, glass and panelling from Europe, teak from Asia and oak and walnut from prime areas of North America. Scottish stonemasons built the wall that surrounds the site. Splendour is evident everywhere: the Conservatory with its elegant bronze doors, Peacock Alley copied and named after the historic hallway in Windsor Castle, the majestic Great Hall with its high ceiling, the Oak Room where artisans worked for three years to fashion the French oak panelling, the Library designed for 100 000 volumes, the luxurious suites once occupied by Sir Henry and Lady Pellatt, a breathtaking view from the battlements, a wine cellar and a hidden staircase which allowed Sir Henry a private retreat from his study.

Developing a Paragraph by Using a Specific Example. Here is a list of topics. Choose one that interests you and develop it into a paragraph through the use of a specific example. You may use a topic of your own.

1. Science fiction becomes fact so quickly it is no longer fiction.
2. A sense of humor can be a valuable tool.
3. Children adopt habits of their peers.
4. A stay in the hospital needn't be a depressing experience.
5. Good friends are loyal, even in a trying situation.
6. We should all learn lessons from history.

Sence of humor is just like medicine, People say that that the more you laugh, the longer you'll live. Infact it is a great way of exercising. If you laugh 20 minutes a day it is equivilent to a 30 minute run. A good way to laugh is to go to a comedy club, watch T.V. or just hang with your friends because you are bound to laugh. So whenever in doubt, laugh out!

Using an Incident or Anecdote   26

Although it is usually limited to such types of writing as inspirational pieces and self-help articles, the **incident or anecdote,** when used sparingly, can add a personal touch to almost any form of writing. The strength of this type of development lies in the fact that the incident or anecdote, if well chosen, can drive a point home very sharply and imprint the idea very clearly in the reader's mind.

There is a similarity between using an example and using an incident or anecdote. The difference is that the paragraph developed by incident or anecdote focuses on an individual incident drawn from personal experience, while the paragraph developed by an example is often impersonal.

Notice how the following example uses an incident drawn from the writer's personal experience:

> One of the most terrifying experiences of my life made me realize how dependent we are upon our vision. I was driving to work in the morning; the sun shone brightly, and I felt relaxed behind the wheel of the car. I had taken the same route to work every morning for the past three years and didn't have to think too seriously about directing the car to my office. As I turned the bend in the road at the lake, I was momentarily blinded by the rising sun glaring off the placid water. With my vision thus obliterated, I completely lost control of the car. I could not negotiate the curve. I could not seem to remember whether I was in the inner or outer lane. I could not recall if there was a divider between me and the oncoming traffic. I could not seem to find the brake pedal. In essence, I panicked! Within seconds I had passed the point of the blinding glare and was able to see again. I was suddenly very conscious of the many everyday sights that usually guided me on my way to work. I realized that without eyesight, even the most routine maneuvers were impossible; my entire world was lost when I could not see. And so it must be, but on a larger scale, for those who lose their sight permanently.

Developing a Paragraph by Using an Incident or Anecdote. Here is a list of topic sentences that may be developed by an incident or anecdote. Choose two of the sentences that interest you. Then, using your own paper, draw from your personal experience and develop each into a paragraph.

1. I have come to the conclusion that I like to work.
2. Getting lost with someone teaches you a lot about him or her.
3. You can find out what people think of you when you ask them for help.
4. Not being invited to a friend's party can make you feel terrible.
5. Visiting someone in the hospital can be an upsetting experience.
6. Caring for a pet can teach you a lot about yourself.
7. Learning to swim was an experience I will never forget.
8. Observing poverty first-hand is an enlightening experience.
9. Being alone doesn't have to be lonely.
10. It pays to be honest with yourself.

Using Comparisons or Contrasts   27

In developing a topic sentence by **comparisons or contrasts,** you will also be using facts, examples, or incidents. The important point to remember here, however, is that you are explaining the *differences* or *similarities* in the facts or ideas. Look at the following example of a paragraph developed by comparison:

> There are some striking similarities between high schools and universities. Both serve as institutes of learning. Students prepare for the future whether in the Arts, Computer Sciences, Medical or Social fields. Homework is a necessity if one is to attain a high standard, and examinations are a must to determine a student's progress. Considering the age-difference between high school and university students, the likenesses are thought-provoking!

The writer's main point was to compare the differences between high schools and universities.

Now, here is an example of a paragraph developed by contrast.

> They were both dogs, but there the similarity ended. Fritzie the Mexican Chihuahua was as small as a pocket. He squeaked when he should have barked. Olga, the great Dane, stood higher than every table in the house. When she barked, the dishes rattled, and Fritzie catapulted straight up into your lap.

It is obviously the writer's intention to contrast the two dogs. They are contrasted specifically in terms of their size and their barks.

Developing a Paragraph by Using Comparisons or Contrasts. Following is a list of topics that may be developed through comparisons or contrasts. Decide on the better method of development for each topic (comparison or contrast). Choose two of the topics that interest you and develop each into a paragraph. You may need to do research on some of the topics.

1. The athlete and the ballet dancer
2. A musician and a mechanic
3. Modern Canadian teenagers and ancient oriental teens
4. Urban life today and rural life of the 1850's
5. The Prime Minister of Canada and the British Prime Minister
6. Soccer and football
7. The coach and an expectant father
8. Cotton and polyester
9. A modern flight to Europe and a sea voyage in the 1700's
10. Movies of the 1980's and movies of the 1970's

Giving Reasons

Sometimes you may have an opinion, an idea, a feeling that you cannot prove with specific facts or statistics. You may have reasoned the opinion through for yourself and reached a conclusion. In writing a paragraph developed by **reasons,** your purpose is to persuade your reader of the rationality of your opinion. Your topic sentence will be a statement of your opinion, and the remainder of the paragraph will give your reasons for arriving at that opinion.

Read the following example of a paragraph developed by reasons:

> Teenagers should earn their own spending money, rather than have it given to them by their parents. If teens work for their money, they are more responsible in spending it. They are encouraged to make adult decisions about the value of time, the value of learning skills, the value of a dollar, and the value of sought-after commodities. The teen who toils also learns the lesson that no one is entitled to a free ride in our society— that a person is entitled to partake of the goods offered in the market place only when he or she has offered a useful service to the economy in a capable manner. It is a benefit to society as well as to the individual teenager when the young person works to earn purchasing power.

It is obvious that the writer thinks that teens must work for their allowance. The writer has several opinions; notice how these are different from *facts* as dealt with on the preceding pages. There is no proof offered here—just the writer's reasons for thinking his or her opinion is valid. There is, of course, an opposite point of view, which could also be developed into a paragraph supported by reasons.

Developing a Paragraph by Giving Reasons. In the space below, write a paragraph that expresses your opinion on a topic of your choice. Develop your opinion by giving reasons that build a sound argument.

Review: Writing Effective Paragraphs 29

Answer the following questions based on the information presented in this chapter.

1. What are the two functions of the topic sentence?

_____

_____

2. How is unity achieved in a paragraph?

_____

3. What should determine the length of a paragraph?

_____

Below are topics that could be developed into paragraphs. For each topic, write a topic sentence. Then, decide which would be the best way of developing the paragraph. Choose from:

facts or statistics   comparisons or contrasts
specific example   reasons
incident or anecdote

Explain your reasons for your choice of method of development. Your reason is important, because some paragraphs could be developed well by more than one method.

1. Speed limit and traffic fatalities

TOPIC SENTENCE _____

_____

METHOD OF DEVELOPMENT _____

REASONS _____

_____

2. The importance of doing things with one's family

TOPIC SENTENCE _____

_____

METHOD OF DEVELOPMENT _____

REASONS _____

_____

3. Canadian schools in the 1980's and Canadian schools in the 1780's

TOPIC SENTENCE _____

_____

METHOD OF DEVELOPMENT _____

REASONS _____

_____

The Narrative Paragraph

The **narrative** paragraph is the simplest and most natural form of writing. It may be based upon fact, imagination, or a combination of both.

Usually written in chronological order, the narrative paragraph is the telling of events.

Because a narrative paragraph does not have to be as carefully constructed as other kinds of paragraphs, you may find that it does not always have a topic sentence. It is best, however, to practice writing paragraphs with topic sentences.

Read the following narrative paragraph. Notice how the topic sentence is developed into a "story" which is written in chronological order.

> The hardest part about going to the dentist is waiting in his or her outer office. After checking in, you find a corner seat and riffle through the three-year-old magazines. Articles pop out on inoculations of tender gums and special drills for deep root canal work. The seconds grow thick and the minutes stagnate heavily in the air. Periodically, strange names are called by the nurse in a strained, impatient voice. The victims jump as if a nerve is struck. They shuffle reluctantly to the gaping door. Closing your eyes against the blaring third-degree fluorescent lights, you see the instruments the dentist uses in garish colors and threatening shapes. But the semidarkness soothes the eyes and rests the nerves—a little too well. Awakened by the nurse's cold hand and scalpel voice, you hear her say that you slept through your appointment. Come back next week—same place, same kind of slow time.

Writing a Narrative Paragraph. Choose one of the topics from the list below that interests you or choose a topic of your own. Develop it into a narrative paragraph. Be sure that you start with a topic sentence that gives focus to your narrative.

1. Your first day of high school
2. The time you helped build something
3. The time you got lost
4. The time you learned a lesson
5. The day you wished you were someone else
6. Your closest brush with death

_____

_____

_____

_____

_____

_____

_____

_____

_____

_____

_____

The Descriptive Paragraph

In writing good **descriptive** paragraphs, you must choose your words carefully and decide on precise details in order to paint a word picture that appeals to your reader's senses.

Notice how the following paragraph appeals to the reader's senses:

> With a smell like burning popcorn the fire awoke him at 4 a.m. A thick oily smoke filled the room. Orange flames flared up the wall. Smoke cottoned his mouth and nostrils choking him. He coughed. The television set was burning! Its plastic antenna was melted down the blackened face of the screen. Dozens of flames fingered out of the set like demons' hands reaching out of a grave for escape. Leaping from his bed, he pulled out the TV cord from the wall. He threw the heavy blanket on top of the fire. His eyes blistered into tears from the smoke. With each movement the blanket was seared into a scorched and smoky mass of gaseous cloth. After dozens of attempts, he stamped out the final flickers on the musty rug. Flinging open the window, he let the slimy smoke ooze outside into the morning air. For ten minutes he coughed and wheezed. Exhausted, he paused. From a far-off other world came a breeze that moistened his nostrils and brought the dewy morning into the room.

Another paragraph may appeal to your sense of touch, as in this example:

> Having waited too long in the day, the scoutmaster had to light his own fire in the suddenly darkened woods. He fumbled for his large box of wooden wind matches. Slivers stuck his fingertips as he pulled the box from the warm pocket of his parka. Wind slid the box through his fingers to crack on a rock at his feet. Crouching, he searched among the twigs, dirt, and insects with rigid fingers. His boy scouts had already built and lighted fires the Indian way. They watched the hunched shadow of their scoutmaster stirring the dust into billows of smoke. They pressed their mouths hard trying not to laugh.

Many paragraphs will appeal to a combination of senses. The important point is that you must choose details carefully in order to paint your word picture.

Writing a Descriptive Paragraph. Choose one of the following topics and develop it into a descriptive paragraph. Be sure that you choose your words and details carefully to appeal to the reader's senses and that you follow a logical order in your description.

1. A passing parade
2. A volleyball game
3. A roller coaster ride
4. A field of flowers
5. A storm
6. Your room
7. A family dinner
8. Catching a fish
9. A swim in the lake
10. Looking for a lost object

The Explanatory Paragraph   32

The **explanatory paragraph** does just what its name implies—it *explains*. The explanatory paragraph can use facts or statistics, specific examples, an incident or an anecdote, comparisons or contrasts, or reasons.

To be meaningful, the information in the explanatory paragraph must be clear, accurate, and well organized. The easiest way to organize explanatory material is to do it in chronological order; that is, first things first.

The following paragraph about the "mudskipper" is an explanatory paragraph developed with facts. Notice how carefully the author arranged the facts to give an accurate and vivid explanation of how the mudskipper maneuvers.

> Any fish that can climb trees would have to be called unique. The mudskipper, a tiny fish of Southeast Asia, can millimeter up the pencil stems of the mangrove tree. The mudskipper's stubby, leg-like chest fins reach ever upward with suction cups while its pelvic fins grip the moist stem. As the pectoral fins grasp the stem, the back fins let go and hunch upward. Its eyes blink and rotate downward periodically into liquid stored at the bottom of its eye sockets. By such devices, the mudskipper can stay out of water for as long as half a day. By filling its gill tanks with a mixture of water and air, it can moisten its gills for breathing on land hours at a time. But, if it climbs trees, why is it called a mudskipper? Its lesser claim to distinction is the fact that from a flat muddy surface it can leap as high as 2 decimeters—twice its own length. While soaring in the air, it flaps its back dorsal fins. So if you owned a mudskipper for your aquarium at home, you could watch it climb the glass.

The following explanatory paragraph is developed by examples:

> Hollywood and history do not always agree on the facts. How many movies have you seen with dinosaurs chasing people? Actually, dinosaurs were a vanished species long before people were available to be chased. How many films have shown Romans riding their chariots roughshod over their enemies in the heat of battle? Actually, the Romans used chariots for cargo, pleasure, and sporting events, but not for battle. How often have you seen King Arthur and his knights at the Round Table when actually there is very little proof of either? Despite the differences over facts between Hollywood and history, the films keep happily rolling on.

Writing Explanatory Paragraphs. On a separate sheet of paper, write an explanatory paragraph that explains a topic with which you are familiar. Organize your information in a clear, accurate manner.

The Persuasive Paragraph

The purpose of a **persuasive paragraph** is to try to persuade or convince others that they ought to believe or act as you wish them to believe or act. The very fact that you make the attempt to persuade implies that there are at least two ways of believing or acting in regard to the matter with which you are concerned. To be effective in your attempt to persuade, study and understand both sides of the problem, as much as you can, no matter what you are advocating. Then, use every device at your disposal to state your arguments honestly and fairly.

The topic sentence of a persuasive paragraph should be stated in the form of a definite proposition, that is, a clear, exact statement of your conclusion. The remainder of your paragraph will then give facts, examples, or reasons to support a *what* and a *why*. The *what* is the proposition; the *why* contains the reasons you give to persuade your reader to believe in the *what*.

Read the following example of a persuasive paragraph and determine *what* the proposition is and *why* the author believes as he or she does about it.

It is about time that schools got back to the basics of "reading, writing, and arithmetic," and stopped wasting time on high-interest electives. High school graduates must be able to read, write, and do basic mathematics before they can be concerned with such advanced concerns as "the role of women in society," "consumerism," and "popular culture," all of which are examples of non-essential courses offered in public schools today. The roles of women and men are irrelevant if neither women nor men are literate. The concept of consumerism becomes meaningless if the consumer can't add or subtract. Popular culture is lowered to the lowest offerings on the "boob tube" if the populace is not equipped with techniques of reading and communicating to elevate it above the most passive role. Come on, teachers and administrators, get in there and teach those 3 R's!

Writing Persuasive Paragraphs. Choose one of the topics from the list below and develop a persuasive paragraph about it. Make sure your topic sentence states your proposition and that the remainder of the paragraph tells why you feel as you do. You may choose a topic of your own.

1. People who are suspected of a crime should be imprisoned immediately.
2. No private citizen should be allowed to own a handgun.
3. Public schools should be in session twelve months a year.
4. Cigarette smoking should be banned in public places.

Review: Types of Paragraphs

Read the following narrative paragraph.

Twice a year my family goes through a national ritual we call Fall Behind and Spring Ahead. First, one autumn evening we, along with most Canadians, will move clocks one hour behind to revert to standard time. The next day, we will argue about who moved which clocks how many times and in what directions. Some appointments will be missed, arguments will ensue, and tempers will flare. Outside authorities will be needed to verify the so-called "real" time. Then, later, apologies will follow, and, afterwards, the confused clocks will be corrected. In a matter of months, however, this ritual will be repeated—but in reverse. Then time will be moved ahead one hour in the spring to permit Daylight Saving Time. So for most Canadians— including my family—it will be spring ahead and fall behind. But, for some obscure reason, parts of the country still insist on staying faithful to nature's own time and so miss participation in this national pastime.

1. How is this paragraph different from explanatory or persuasive paragraphs?

_____

2. What is the purpose of this narrative?

_____

_____

Read the following descriptive paragraph.

As he bit into the triple-deck ice cream cone, his teeth ached with cold pleasure. A wet numbness pierced his mouth. His tongue curved the chocolate into spirals blending with vanilla into soft marble. He pressed the strawberry down hard until his tongue hurt. Melting ice cream rainbowed slowly down the cone to sticky fingers. He licked the dry, corrugated cone held in his warm, moist hand.

1. How is this paragraph different from explanatory or persuasive paragraphs?

_____

2. What is the purpose of this description?

_____

_____

The Subject for a Composition

A composition is a group of closely related paragraphs dealing with a single topic or idea. Usually, one paragraph, called the **introductory paragraph,** states the main idea of the composition. All the other paragraphs relate to this introductory paragraph and further explain or support the main idea.

Deciding On a Subject. In making your decision as to what to write about, you should consider the two most important sources of information available to you: (1) *yourself,* and (2) *others.*

By using yourself as a subject for a composition, you can draw from your own uniqueness, your own experiences, your own individuality.

In going beyond yourself for subjects to write about, you may use many different sources. You may interview someone who has had an interesting experience. You may consult an authority in a certain area. You can make use of the entire field of published material, gaining information wherever possible. In order to write knowledgeably about a subject, you must gain more information about the subject than the average individual has. After you get an idea for a topic for a composition, it is wise to consult the library to see just how much information is available.

Narrowing the Subject. In order for an idea to be treated adequately and satisfactorily within the limits of the paragraph, the idea must be narrowed. Here is a three-step method for narrowing a topic you may be considering for a composition:

1. List the topic
2. Write a general topic statement or question
3. Write a specific topic sentence

TOPIC   Insects
GENERAL TOPIC QUESTION   Where do butterflies go in winter?
SPECIFIC SENTENCE   Monarch butterflies spend the winter in the safety of Mexico's Sierra Madre Mountains.

Choosing and Narrowing a Subject. Choose five of the following topics and narrow each topic by proceeding from topic to general topic statement or question, to specific sentence. Determine whether each should be developed with *you* as a subject or with *others* as a subject. Where research would be necessary, do a preliminary library search to see how much information will be available to you on the subject. Save your work to use in the next exercise.

Illusions	Superstitions
Explorers	Books
Medicine	Rituals
Astronomy	Reptiles
Inventions	Art

Planning a Composition

Once you have chosen your topic and appropriately narrowed it, you must begin your planning. Preliminary planning should include a decision as to your audience (for whom the writing is intended) and the purpose of your composition (what you wish to do for your audience—entertain them, inform them, etc.). Decisions such as these will dictate the type of material you will seek and the tone in which you will present it.

Putting Down Ideas. As you begin to plan your composition, jot down ideas you may already have on 7.5 x 12.5 cm cards. As you do your reading, jot down additional ideas. There need be no organization to your ideas at this point, merely list all ideas which are within the limits of your subject.

Grouping Ideas. Once you have made as complete a list of ideas as you can, both from your own thoughts and from your research, you must begin grouping ideas. You need to organize ideas in relation to one another. Try to determine major ideas—those that encompass many smaller ideas. Think about how the ideas can be grouped together and try to put ideas into three major groupings. This will be a manageable amount for a student composition. Each major idea should have sufficient sub-ideas to develop and support it.

Planning by Putting Down and Grouping Ideas. Refer to your list of five topic sentences from the previous exercise. Now, choose one that you wish to develop into a composition. Begin by making a list of ideas that relate to your topic. Then, group your ideas into approximately three major ideas, with supporting ideas or related ideas beneath them.

If your topic were "Rituals," for example, you would proceed like this:

TOPIC STATEMENT OR QUESTION   What is an unusual ritual?

TOPIC SENTENCE   Have you ever heard of the natives of the South Pacific who tie vines to their ankles and leap from towers 24.38 metres high?

IDEAS

description of the dive itself	how children imitate the dive
origin of the dive	building the tower
location of the tribe	preparing the ground
description of tower	guarding the tower
personal preparation of diver	purposes of the ritual
role of women	

GROUPING THE IDEAS   You should be able to group the above ideas into main groups dealing with:

1. The Dive Itself
2. Preparation for the Dive
3. Origin of the Dive

When you have listed your ideas and grouped them, you will be ready to make your working outline.

Making a Working Outline

The final step in organizing your ideas is to make a **working outline.** Because you already have all your ideas for the body of your composition in related groups, this final step is not difficult. You are merely going to reorganize your ideas into a logical order.

There are several different ways a composition can be organized; each subject presents an organizational pattern of its own. Some compositions may be organized chronologically; other topics may be organized in order of importance. Another organizational pattern is to go from the familiar to the unfamiliar. Whatever the plan you choose for your topic, the important thing to remember about outlining is that it is to help your ideas move in a logical direction.

Here is a sample of a working outline for the composition on the divers who tie the vines around their ankles:

I. Origin of Dive
    A. Man mistreated his wife
    B. Wife ran away and climbed banyan tree
    C. Man climbed after her
    D. She tied vines around her ankles
    E. She jumped, he fell
    F. Vines saved her life
    G. Husband died
    H. Friends began practicing dives to regain pride

II. Preparation for the Dive
    A. Construction of high diving tower by divers themselves
        1. Select strong tree
        2. Add support poles
        3. Gather logs and thick branches
        4. Use four kilometres of vines, no nails, no wire
        5. Takes ten days to construct
    B. Personal Preparation
        1. Wash in sea
        2. Rub bodies with coconut oil
        3. Decorate bodies
        4. Carry boars' tusks

III. The Dive
    A. Natives take turns tying vines to both ankles
    B. Diver gives speech to natives below
    C. The diver leaps off platform
    D. He plummets to earth
    E. Vines break fall as diver's head rakes dirt
    F. Other men untie vines and congratulate diver

Making a Working Outline. Now, make a working outline for your composition. Determine an overall plan of logical organization, and then rearrange your ideas from your list on the preceding page in logical, outline form.

The Introductory Paragraph

Your groundwork is now finished. Your topic is selected, your audience and purpose decided on, your information organized into a logical pattern of development. You are now ready to organize and begin writing your composition.

In defining the composition, we said: "A composition is a group of closely related paragraphs dealing with a single topic or idea. Usually one paragraph, called the **introductory paragraph,** states the main idea of the composition. All the other paragraphs must be related to this introductory paragraph. These paragraphs further explain or support the main idea." To this definition we now need to add: "A good composition always contains a beginning, a middle, and an end." A composition should contain:

I. The Introductory Paragraph

II. The Body

    A. Supporting information   (The information in

    B. Supporting information   your working outline.)

    C. Supporting information

III. The Conclusion

The introductory paragraph of your composition serves two important functions and must, therefore, be written with great care. First, a good introductory paragraph catches the reader's attention. Second, it gives the reader an idea as to what the composition is about.

You can write the introductory paragraph as a *direct appeal,* in which you simply explain your main idea. You can use a *personal approach* in which you either speak directly to the reader as "you," or speak in a personal tone, yourself, as "I." You can also write an introductory paragraph that is a *description of an overall effect,* which you will develop in the remainder of the composition. Or, you can write a paragraph that is a *question or statement that arouses the reader's curiosity.*

Whatever approach you use, remember that the purpose of the introductory paragraph is to attract your reader, to give your reader an indication of what your subject is, and to limit the subject matter of your composition.

Here is a sample introductory paragraph for the composition about the divers. Notice how the author uses a question to arouse the reader's interest.

> Have you ever heard of the natives in the South Pacific who tie vines to their ankles and leap from towers 24.38 metres high? As the divers fall to within a body's distance of the earth, the vines yank them heels over head, swinging them into a mound of earth so that their foreheads scrape the soil. How did this unusual ritual get started?

Writing the Introductory Paragraph. Now write the introductory paragraph for your composition.

The Body

The **body** is the major part of the composition. The ideas indicated in the introductory paragraph are further developed or explained. There are two important points to note about the body of the composition: it is always divided into paragraphs that correspond to the main topics in your working outline; and each paragraph of the composition usually begins with a topic sentence.

In order to give the composition a feeling of **unity,** a feeling that everything is tied together and is not merely a series of isolated ideas, the good writer makes use of **transitional devices.** These devices tie the ideas of the composition together by referring both to the idea that precedes and the idea that will follow. Here are six basic transitional devices:

USING WORDS THAT INDICATE TIME   after, meanwhile, today, next

USING WORDS THAT SHOW RELATIONSHIP BETWEEN IDEAS   also, because, therefore, similarly

USING WORDS THAT SHOW AN OPPOSITE POINT OF VIEW   but, on the other hand, yet, while, however

REPEATING WORDS USED EARLIER

USING SYNONYMS FOR WORDS USED EARLIER

USING PRONOUNS THAT REFER TO WORDS USED EARLIER

Underline the transitional devices used within these paragraphs.

1.   On the other hand, southpaws enjoy an advantage in baseball. When they bat, they are two steps closer to first base than right-handed hitters. They own the first-base position. They are called upon to relieve right-handed pitchers when the batter is a lefty. However, they can play any outfield position. In contrast to a right-hander, they don't have to worry about becoming a catcher with swollen knuckles. Although righties are in the privileged majority in the stands, lefties, by contrast, are a priceless minority on the field. Lefties truly succeed—on their other hand.

2.   Even though some men didn't understand, she insisted on using Ms. anyway. Some thought she was being defiant toward traditional society. Some thought she was divorced; others thought she was looking. Some viewed her as indecisive or as liberated. But not Ms., herself. She did not think of herself as a label at all. She thought of herself as an individual person. She used Ms. because it was more accurate.

3.   Everyone has roots. Every people has beginnings. The answer lies in questions. Do we know those beginnings? Can we trace those roots? Can those answers become ropes we can use to climb slowly out of the well of isolated uniqueness? Everyone is a root. What we need to do is track the soil back to the trunk of our shared experiences. For what are roots without the tree of humankind?

Writing the Body of the Composition. Using your working outline for the topic you have chosen, write the body of your composition. Try to achieve unity through the use of transitional devices.

The Conclusion

The final step in writing the composition is to write the **conclusion.** The concluding paragraph ties all the ideas together and indicates to the reader that you are finished.

There are many appropriate ways to conclude a composition. Some conclusions repeat ideas from the introductory paragraph, while other conclusions summarize. Some writers return to the direct appeal, while others use personal approach. Whatever method you choose to conclude your composition, make certain it reinforces your purpose and ties your ideas together into a unified, completed work.

Concluding the Composition. Now you are ready to complete your composition. Much of the work has already been done and simply needs to be put in final form. Follow the steps below to organize your work.

1. Write your subject here: _____

2. Write your topic statement or question here: _____

   _____

3. Write your topic sentence here: _____

   _____

4. Write your introductory paragraph here: _____

   _____

   _____

   _____

   _____

   _____

5. On a separate sheet of paper, write your working outline, which will group together in logical order all of your ideas.

6. Write the body of your composition on a separate piece of paper, but write the topic sentences for each paragraph of the composition here:

   _____

   _____

   _____

   _____

7. Write your conclusion here:

   _____

   _____

   _____

   _____

8. Reread your entire composition and revise it as necessary.

The Forms of Letters 41

Business letters always contain the following information, in this order:

1. The **heading** contains your address (street address on one line, city and province on the second line, postal code on the third line) and the date.

2. The **inside address** includes the person or department to whom you are writing on the first line; the name of the company on the second line; the street address (or post office box number) on the third line; the city and province on the fourth line, and the postal code on the fifth line. One space is left blank between the inside address and the next part, the salutation.

3. The **salutation** will depend on the person to whom you are writing. You may write: "Dear Sir or Madam:" or "Dear Ms. Bell:" etc. A blank space is left between the salutation of the letter and the body.

4. The **body** is the most important part of your letter. This is where you state your purpose. A blank space is left between the body and the closing.

5. The **closing** may be "Sincerely," "Yours truly," "Cordially," and so on. Only the first word of the closing is capitalized, and it is always followed by a comma.

6. Your **signature** is written beneath the closing. Type your name below your signature.

The envelope. Envelopes contain two items:

1. The **return address** is placed in the upper left-hand corner. Include your name on the first line; your street address on the second line; your city and province on the third line; and your postal code on the fourth line.

2. The **address** of the place to which you are sending the letter is placed in the middle of the envelope. Simply copy the inside address here.

Writing Business Letters and Envelopes. Practice writing a business letter on your own paper, as indicated below. Address an "envelope" as well.

1. Write to Harold Daws, Executive Editor, *Canadian Consumer* magazine, and request a test report on a bicycle (specify the name of the bike you are interested in and the information you want—i.e., price, dealers etc.) The address of the company is 3892 Yonge St., Toronto, Ontario M4N 3R5.

2. Write a nearby trade school or college and request a catalogue of classes and information about admissions.

3. Write a letter to a local business and ask about part-time help. Describe yourself, and tell what type of job you are interested in.

Requests for Information

The one type of business letter you will use more than any other is the request for information. The body of the letter should be brief, with the main emphasis on what information you need and why you need it. Always be specific.

Letters requesting information may seek material for a school report. Other letters may be about employment. Letters about employment must include specific facts, such as the type of job you are interested in and any previous experience you have had. State clearly whether you are looking for full-time, part-time, or temporary employment. State your age, grade in school, and the date you will be available for work.

Writing a Letter Requesting Information. Write a letter in which you ask for material for a report, for a job interview, or for information from a school. Follow the proper business letter format.

Applications

Fill in the items on this application form completely. Print neatly.

Personal Information

Date   Social Insurance Number

Name   Age   Sex

                Last   First   Middle

Present Address

                    Street   City   Province   Postal Code

Phone Number   Date of Birth   Canadian Citizen   Yes   No

Employment Desired

Position   Date You Can Start   Salary Desired

Are You Employed Now?   Where?   Duties

Education

	Name and Location of School	Years Attended	Date Graduated	Subjects Studied
Elementary School				
High School				
College or Trade School				
Canadian Military or Naval Service	Rank			
Activities Other Than Religious (Civic, Athletic, etc.)				

Former Employers *(List Below Last Two Employers, Starting With More Recent One)*

Dates	Name and Address of Employer	Salary	Position	Reason for Leaving
From To				
From To				

References: *(Give Below the Names of Two Persons Not Related To You, Whom You Have Known At Least One Year.*

Name	Address	Business

List Any Physical Defects   Were You Ever Injured?

In Case of Emergency Notify

                    Name   Address   Phone No.

I authorize investigation of all statements contained in this application. I understand that misrepresentation or omission of facts called for is cause for dismissal.

Date   Signature

Résumés

A **résumé** is a personal inventory of your life as it applies to a career. The form below is one that can be followed in writing a résumé. It tells you what important information is to be included, and how it can be organized.

RÉSUMÉ

Name Street address
City, and Province
Postal code
Telephone number

Objective Describe type of job you are seeking.

Experience List where you have worked before, most recent job first. For each job, supply:
    Period employed
    Name and address of firm
    Position held
    Duties

Education List all schools attended, starting with most recent. For each school, list:
    Name of school
    Place of school
    Special subjects

Personal List these items:
    Place and date of birth
    Marital status
    Health
    Professional memberships
    Activities; hobbies or special interests
    Special skills

References Give names and addresses of people who know you or for whom you have worked, and who will give you good recommendations.

Here are some guidelines for writing a résumé:

1. Use 21.5 x 28 cm white paper.
2. Type your résumé or have it typed.
3. Proofread carefully.
4. Be brief. Complete sentences are not necessary, since this is a compilation of facts. A résumé should be no longer than two pages.

Preparing a Résumé. Take a sheet of paper and write a rough draft of a résumé for yourself. Give careful thought to items to be included, and how they should best be phrased.

Review: Letters, Applications, and Résumés

In the space below, write a letter to a local business requesting an application for employment.

_____

_____

_____

_____

_____

_____

_____

_____

_____

_____

_____

_____

_____

_____

_____

_____

_____

_____

Write a résumé to accompany the above letter.

_____

_____

_____

_____

_____

_____

_____

_____

_____

_____

_____

_____

_____

_____

_____

_____

_____

_____

How Books Are Classified and Arranged

Fiction. Novels and short story collections are usually arranged in alphabetical order by author. For example, a book by John Steinbeck will be under *S*.

Nonfiction. Most libraries classify nonfiction books according to the Dewey Decimal System. Books are classified by number in ten major categories, according to their subjects. The ten major Dewey categories are:

000-099	**General Works** (encyclopedias, references, almanacs, etc.)
100-199	**Philosophy**
200-299	**Religion**
300-399	**Social Science**
400-499	**Language**
500-599	**Science**
600-699	**Applied Sciences**
700-799	**Fine Arts**
800-899	**Literature**
900-999	**History** (including biography)

The major categories are subdivided into many more specific classifications. Each nonfiction book is assigned a number within the major category.

Nonfiction books are arranged on the shelves numerically in order of their classification. Within each classification, books are arranged alphabetically by authors' last names.

Classifying Books. Below are titles and authors of five fiction books. Put them in order as they would appear in the library.

The Great Gatsby by F. Scott Fitzgerald
Wuthering Heights by Emily Brontë
Deenie by Judy Blume
The Red Pony by John Steinbeck
Durango Street by Frank Bonham

1. _____
2. _____
3. _____
4. _____
5. _____

How the Dewey Decimal System Classifies Information. In what major category would books on the following topics be found?

1. Judaism _____
2. Beethoven's symphonies _____
3. The romantic poets _____
4. Customs of an Indian tribe _____
5. Development of the English language _____

The Card Catalogue

The **card catalogue** is an index to all books in the library. It contains alphabetically arranged cards, each of which bears the title of a book located in the library. In the upper left-hand corner of each card is the **call number**, or classification number of the book. This call number will help you locate the book on the shelves.

There are usually three cards for the same book in the card catalogue. The **author card** bears the author's name on the top line (last name first) and is thus filed alphabetically by author. The **title card** for the same book will have the title of the book on the top line. The place of the title card in the catalogue is determined by the first letter of the first word in the title. (*A*, *An*, and *The* do not count as first words.) The **subject card** for the same book will have the name of the topic of the book on its top line.

Card Information. All three types of catalogue cards give information that includes

1. The call number,
2. The title, author, publisher, and date of publication,
3. The number of pages, and a notation on whether the book has illustrations, maps, tables, or other features.

Often the catalogue card will also provide

1. A brief description of the nature and scope of this book,
2. A listing of other catalogue cards for the book.

Other Helpful Information. You will also find **guide cards** in the card catalogue. They each have a tab that projects above the other cards. They offer guide words (general subject headings) to aid you in finding other catalogue cards quickly.

Cross reference cards refer you to other subject headings closely related to the one in which you are interested. The cards will say "See" or "See Also" and then a subject or list of subjects.

Using the Card Catalogue. List the title, author, call number, and publication date of all books about two of the following people. Use your own paper.

1. Lester Pearson
2. Helen Keller
3. Governor General Schreyer
4. Henry VIII
5. Mayor Drapeau

List subject cards that would give you information about two of the following subjects.

1. Automobile engines
2. The Senate
3. Agricultural procedures
4. The United Nations
5. Crop dusting

Using Reference Works (I)

Reference works are tools for obtaining information; like tools, they should be used in definite ways. Before using any reference work for the first time, you would be wise to skim the preface, which will describe how information is arranged, show sample entries, and explain symbols and abbreviations used in the book.

Some basic types of reference works are

1. **Dictionaries.** Dictionaries may be classified as three major types: unabridged (complete) containing more than 500 000 words; abridged (shorter) editions; and pocket-sized. There are also dictionaries that deal with specific aspects of the English language, such as synonyms and antonyms, slang, rhymes, etc.

2. **Encyclopedias.** Encyclopedias are collections of articles, alphabetically arranged. There are general encyclopedias which contain articles on nearly every subject known. There are many special-purpose encyclopedias dealing with a specific subject, such as sports, archaeology, Indian culture, etc.

3. **Almanacs and Yearbooks.** Almanacs and yearbooks are published annually and are the most useful sources of facts and statistics on current events, government, economics, sports, and other fields.

4. **Biographical References.** Biographical references are books that offer information about the lives of important people. They often deal with people who can be grouped together into one classification, such as authors or politicians.

5. **Books About Authors.** There are many informative books of biographies that deal exclusively with famous authors, such as *European Authors: 1000-1900*; *Twentieth Century Authors*, and so on.

Using Reference Works. List below the names of at least three dictionaries found in your school or public library.

1. _____
2. _____
3. _____

Find at least three encyclopedia articles dealing with "cancer." List the name of the encyclopedia, the volume in which the article appears, and the page number of each article. Also, note the copyright dates of the encyclopedias consulted.

1. _____
2. _____
3. _____

Use any of the above-mentioned reference works to answer the following questions.

1. When was Wayne Gretsky born? _____
2. Name two books written by Farley Mowat. _____
3. What is the population of China? (most recent census) _____
4. What are three synonyms for *old*? _____
5. How does a barometer work? _____

Using Reference Works (II)   ' **49**

1. **Literary Reference Books.** There are many valuable reference books on the history of literature, on quotations and proverbs, on locating poems and stories, and on finding information about writers. Some are *Bartlett's Familiar Quotations*, *The Oxford Companion to Canadian History and Literature*, and *Granger's Index to Poetry*.

2. **Pamphlets, Handbooks, and Catalogues.** Most libraries have pamphlets, handbooks, booklets, and clippings on a variety of subjects. These are kept in a set of file cabinets called the vertical file.

3. **Atlases.** In addition to containing maps, atlases contain interesting data on a number of subjects. There are even specific-subject atlases, such as *Atlas of World History*, *Atlas of World Wildlife*, and *A Historical Atlas of Canada*.

4. **Magazines.** The *Journal of Canadian Fiction* contains stories and poems and a synopsis of reviews published in Canada. Its purpose is to promote knowledge about Canadian literary activities. Articles are classified under the headings: **Fiction, Canadian Literature/Litterature Canadienne,** and **Biographies.** The *Journal of Canadian Fiction* is a reference work with which you will want to become familiar.

Using Library Reference Works. Using the reference works mentioned above, answer the following questions.

1. What is the population of Edmonton, Alberta? _____

_____

2. What Canadian authors were considered part of the seal hunt in Newfoundland?

_____

3. What is Juliet's famous quotation about what is in a name? (From *Romeo and Juliet*, by William Shakespeare.)

_____

4. In the following listing from the *Journal of Canadian Fiction*, find the asked-for information.

Gom, Leona M. "Margaret Laurence and the First Person" DR LV.2, 236-251

   a. Who wrote the review? _____

   b. What is the title of the article? _____

   c. In what magazine does the article appear? _____

   d. In what section does the article appear? _____

   e. On what page does the article appear? _____

   f. What does LV.2 mean? _____

Review: Using the Library

Answer the following questions about the library:

1. What is the primary reason for using each of the following reference works?

Dictionaries _____

Atlases _____

Canadian Periodical Index _____

Vertical File _____

Almanacs _____

2. Explain how fiction books are arranged on the library shelves.

_____

3. Explain how nonfiction books are arranged on the library shelves.

_____

4. How does the card catalogue help you locate books?

_____

_____

5. What information about each book in the library does the card catalogue offer?

_____

_____

Go to your school or public library and answer the following questions.

1. What are titles of three biographies of Sir John A. Macdonald?

_____

_____

_____

2. What is the Dewey Decimal number for books about jets? _____

3. In what magazine (title, volume, date) did an article about Prime Minister Pierre Trudeau appear in 1977?

_____

4. What are some cross references you can look up to get more information about polio?

_____

5. What is the most recent information your library has about Canadian athletes?

_____

Grammar and Usage

The Noun

A noun is the name of a person, place, or thing.

PERSONS	PLACES	THINGS
girl	town	earth
Lester Pearson	Central Avenue	citizenship

A **common noun** is a name common to a whole group of persons, places or things. A **proper noun** is the name of an individual person, place, or thing and must begin with a capital letter.

COMMON NOUNS	PROPER NOUNS
doctor	Dr. Miller, Judge Olson, Ms. K. Lyle
city	Saskatoon, Atlantic Ocean, New Brunswick
month	February, Tuesday, Veterans' Day

Identifying Nouns. Underline all the nouns in the following sentences.

Example: *Jim* went quickly to the *telephone* and called the *police*.

1. Our house was designed by a local architect, Susan Green.
2. The Dewey Decimal System is used to classify books in a library.
3. Either the Principal or the Vice-Principal will attend the conference in Calgary.
4. Clare Jordan, our secretary, read the minutes of the meeting.
5. Mrs. Johnson serves in the legislature in Winnipeg.
6. Wayne Gretsky plays for the Toronto Maple Leafs.
7. My whole family was able to see the Queen's Plate this year.
8. Dick likes football but finds baseball too slow.
9. John Adams is our Mayor.
10. The artist has several paintings at the exhibit this month.

Common Nouns and Proper Nouns. In the following sentences, decide which nouns are *proper nouns*. Rewrite them, using capital letters.

Example: Every summer he camps near green lake. _Green Lake_

1. The prize will be awarded by duncan campbell-scott. _Duncan Campbell-Scott_
2. My sister will soon graduate from mcgill university. _McGill University_
3. Our friends will soon leave for a tour of italy. _~~Itly~~ Italy_
4. Maria is now a patient at st. boniface general. _Maria, St. Boniface General_
5. My pen pal is a girl who lives in france. _France_
6. We crossed the st. lawrence river soon after noon. _St. Lawrence,_
7. She has never been to australia or new zealand. _Australia, New Zealand_
8. The short story was written by uncle carl. _~~~~ Carl_
9. Our family visited victoria last summer. _Victoria_
10. Let's go to the parade on labour day. _Labour Day_

The Pronoun

A pronoun is a word used in place of a noun. The noun the pronoun refers to is called the **antecedent.**

Personal Pronouns. Pronouns used in place of people's names are called **personal pronouns.** Personal pronouns are also used to refer to things.

FIRST PERSON (the person speaking): I, me, my, mine, we, us, our, ours
SECOND PERSON (the person spoken to): you, your, yours
THIRD PERSON (the person or thing spoken about): he, she, it, they, his, hers, its, their, theirs, him, her, them

Compound Personal Pronouns. A *compound personal pronoun* is formed by adding *-self* or *-selves* to certain personal pronouns, as follows:

FIRST PERSON   myself, ourselves
SECOND PERSON   yourself, yourselves
THIRD PERSON   himself, herself, itself, oneself, themselves

Identifying Personal Pronouns. Underline the personal pronouns. Circle the antecedent of each pronoun and draw an arrow to it.

1. Mr. Black told Kathy that he would give her a summer job in his store.

2. Mr. Nelson listens to news reports on the radio, but they sometimes upset him.

3. David lost his book on Monday, but on Tuesday he found it again.

4. The chef prepared the pepper steak, but it wasn't up to his usual standards.

5. Carlos meant to bring the new flute to rehearsal, but he forgot it.

6. Janet has toured Nova Scotia and New Brunswick, and they have become her favorite provinces.

7. Betty washed the two blankets, and then she hung them out to dry.

8. The members considered the bill carefully before they voted on it.

9. The club members approved the treasurer's report as soon as they heard it.

10. Jill played her flute while Lois played her guitar.

Using Compound Personal Pronouns. Find an acceptable compound personal pronoun for each sentence below. Write it in the space. Then draw an arrow to its antecedent.

Example: We *ourselves* will have to do the clean-up work.

1. Mrs. Miller built the storage cabinet by _herself_.
2. Jane hurt _herself_ when she fell on the gravel.
3. The book _itself_ is full of mystery.
4. He blames _himself_ for the failure of the expedition.
5. We are making our costumes for the play _itself_.

More About Pronouns

Indefinite Pronouns. Some pronouns do not refer to a definite person or thing. The following are called **indefinite pronouns:**

SINGULAR INDEFINITE PRONOUNS

another	anything	either	everything	no one
anybody	one	everyone	neither	someone
anyone	each	everybody	nobody	somebody

PLURAL INDEFINITE PRONOUNS

both   many   few   several

Demonstrative Pronouns. Words like *this, that, these,* and *those* are used to point out which one or ones are meant. They always refer to a definite person or thing, but the words they refer to usually come later.

That is my house. (*house* is the word referred to.)

Interrogative Pronouns. The pronouns *who, whose, whom, which,* and *what* are used to ask questions. When used in this way, they are **interrogative pronouns.**

Who is at the door?

Identifying Pronouns. Decide whether the pronouns underlined in the following sentences are **A** indefinite pronouns, **B** demonstrative pronouns, or **C** interrogative pronouns.

1. <u>Who</u> is the new mayor? _C_
2. <u>No one</u> knows the problem better than Mrs. Smith. _A_
3. <u>Those</u> are not the only hardships the pioneers endured. _B_
4. <u>Each</u> of us wants to do his best on the project. _A_
5. <u>That</u> is a hard question to answer. _B_
6. <u>Whom</u> did you see at the party? _C_
7. <u>Everyone</u> is eager to see that movie. _A_
8. <u>That</u> is the Browns' house over there. _B_
9. <u>Neither</u> of the teams did well this year. _A_
10. <u>Whose</u> are these glasses? _C_
11. <u>Few</u> of the students know what their life work will be. _A_
12. <u>This</u> is my favorite magazine. _B_
13. <u>Whom</u> did you sit by at the play? _C_
14. There isn't <u>anything</u> left in the cupboard. _A_
15. <u>Several</u> of us plan to go to the art show on Sunday. _A_
16. <u>Which</u> of the reference books do you prefer? _C_
17. <u>This</u> is not the sort of game I enjoy. _B_
18. <u>Both</u> of us will be late if we don't hurry. _A_
19. <u>Who</u> plays center on your team? _C_
20. <u>Someone</u> is coming up the sidewalk now. _A_

The Verb

A verb is a word that tells of an action or state of being. The verb tells what is happening in the sentence.

Action verbs are verbs of doing something: *hope, dream, eat, speak*.

I *read* many magazines.   Dolores *ate* the pizza.

Linking verbs describe a state of being. These verbs link the subject to a noun or adjective.

Jim *is* sleepy.   Sue *was* tired.

The word *be* is a linking verb, as are its forms: *am, are, is, was, were, be, been,* and *being*. Other linking verbs are *appear, become, seem, sound, feel, remain,* and *stay*.

Helen *seems* calm.   The children *remained* quiet.

Many linking verbs become action verbs when they describe the *act* of doing something.

I *felt* the soft fabric.

Identifying Action Verbs and Linking Verbs. In the following sentences, underline each verb. Then write **A** if it is an action verb or **L** if it is a linking verb.

Example: Jane feels happy again. __*L*__

1. Joe cooked dinner for the family. __AL__
2. The boy seemed restless after the long program. __L__
3. The popcorn smells good. __L__
4. We stayed quiet for an hour after dinner. __L__
5. Our dog always strains at its leash. __L__
6. Liz Smith pitched for our team in the game yesterday. __L__
7. The pizza tastes good. __L__
8. Eve was president of her graduating class. __L__
9. The boys appear calm again after all the excitement. __L__
10. I play the piano an hour every day. __A__
11. Our new puppy chews everything in sight. __L__
12. The audience grew quiet. __L__
13. Marge stayed quiet after her bout with the flu. __L__
14. The boys feel tired after their long hike. __L__
15. I tasted the hot soup carefully. __A__
16. We grow both flowers and vegetables in our garden. __A__
17. Carla asked her teacher about the exam. __L__
18. Your house seems very large. __A__
19. Which of the two ideas sounds better to you? __L__
20. Jack tripped over the rug. __A__

Main Verbs and Auxiliaries 57

Many verbs consist of more than one word. They consist of a **main verb** and one or more **auxiliaries,** or helping verbs. The last word in the phrase is the main verb.

The most frequently used auxiliaries are the forms of *do, be* and *have.* The most common of the other auxiliaries are the following:

must	may	shall	could	would
might	can	will	should	

AUXILIARY	MAIN VERB	VERB
has	been	has been
is	giving	is giving
should have	played	should have played
could have been	hurt	could have been hurt
was being	used	was being used

Often the parts of a verb are separated by a modifier or modifiers that are not part of the verb.

We *had* just *arrived.* He *will* certainly *recognize* us next time.

Identifying the Complete Verb. Underline the main verb and the auxiliary in the following sentences. Do not include any modifiers.

1. When are you going on your canoe trip?
2. Mr. Costello is constantly giving us directions for each step in our work.
3. Jim should have pitched his tent sooner.
4. Joe could have been badly injured.
5. The new paints are constantly being improved.
6. We will be electing class officers tomorrow.
7. The snowfall had not quite ended at six this morning.
8. I shall certainly miss you next week.
9. Mrs. Barnes has always given generously to charity.
10. The price of most food is rising again.
11. How many books have you read this year?
12. I have already seen that TV program.
13. The old man does not walk to town any more.
14. Nancy and Mark have been given major parts in the school play.
15. Your good deed will never be forgotten.
16. Ms. Smith has definitely agreed to our suggestions.
17. The new club officers will have been chosen by tomorrow evening.
18. You could have gone to the party without me.
19. Mr. Davis has never neglected his work before.
20. Our team could have played in the provincial tournament.

The Adjective

An adjective is a word that modifies a noun or a pronoun. The word *modify* means "to change or add to in some way."

Adjectives are used to tell *which one, what kind, how many,* or *how much* about nouns and pronouns.

WHICH ONE	*this* ball, *that* store, *these* tires, *those* magazines
WHAT KIND	*large* suitcase, *sweet* corn, *dull* program, *beautiful* scene
HOW MANY	*some* apples, *all* cats, *several* choices, *most* students, *five* cars
HOW MUCH	*little* encouragement, *much* help, *plentiful* supply

Three little words —*the, a,* and *an*—are called **articles,** not adjectives.

Identifying Adjectives. In the following sentences, underline each adjective. Then circle the word it describes or modifies and draw an arrow to it.

Example: The green dress is pretty on Betsy.

1. Most new Prime Ministers are cautious when they choose a cabinet.

2. The window of the store was full of attractive new clothes.

3. The red ribbon was given to the best gardener.

4. Several tall boys are members of the team this year.

5. That program is a good comedy.

6. Little work can be done on the project now.

7. The long trip on the famous Orient Express took one from Paris

to Istanbul.

8. Two people can set up camp in a short time.

9. Because she was energetic, Sally jogged for two hours.

10. Some authors attract the attention of the reader with the first paragraph.

11. The new neighbors are friendly.

12. The melon was large and sweet.

13. Joyce is never conceited about winning.

14. A hundred people turned up for the first meeting.

15. Many students study foreign languages.

16. The teacher sounded angry when he spoke to the noisy students.

17. The woman seems worried about finances.

18. Karen is popular with old and young people.

19. Those long questions were hard for me.

20. Much rain fell during the month of June.

The Adverb

The adverb modifies a verb, an adjective, or another adverb. Adverbs tell *where, when, how,* or *to what extent.*

WHERE   Leave your coat *inside.*
WHEN   She arrived *late.*
HOW   He drove *slowly.*
TO WHAT EXTENT   The wall was *completely* covered with vines.

Identifying Adverbs. Read the following sentences carefully. Underline each adverb, and draw an arrow to the word or words it modifies. (Don't forget to include auxiliary verbs as well as the main verb.)

Example: Mary often arrives early for school.

1. Stephen Leacock's books are still widely read.
2. By six o'clock the ground was completely covered with snow.
3. Always work hard.
4. Mr. Jones left his laundry outside in the rain.
5. Susan arrived late for the party.
6. Sarah has worked diligently for her promotion.
7. The little boy fell down on the gravel.
8. Tearfully, the old man put away his treasures.
9. He stepped inside cautiously.
10. Timidly the child raised her hand in class.
11. He is not financially able to buy a house.
12. Mr. Smith is grading our term papers carefully.
13. My cousin will arrive at Mirabel tonight at six o'clock.
14. If no one answers the door, leave quickly.
15. Mrs. Brown gazed sadly out the window.
16. Sit down quickly before class begins.
17. He drove slowly as he approached the intersection.
18. I shall gladly help you.
19. Joan always memorizes her part easily.
20. Dick secretly longed to be a hero.

The Preposition

A preposition relates its object to some other word in the sentence.

A preposition never appears alone. It is always used with a word or group of words called its **object.**

> Go *into* the house. (*into* is a preposition; *house* is its object.)
> Mrs. Jones fell *off* the ladder. (*off* is a preposition; *ladder* is its object.)

Here are some frequently used prepositions:

about	among	beside	except	near	through
above	around	between	for	of	to
across	at	beyond	from	off	under
after	before	by	in	on	up
against	behind	down	into	out	with
along	beneath	during	like	over	without

Identifying Prepositions and Their Objects. Underline each preposition in the following sentences, and draw an arrow to its object. Remember, there are many more prepositions than those listed above.

Example: Joe left his jacket at my house.

1. It rained hard during the night.
2. The boy climbed carefully up the tree.
3. Mary and Betty were the best golfers on the team.
4. I'd like a red jacket like yours.
5. Our basketball team will play against yours tonight.
6. They live in the Eastern Townships across the St. Lawrence River.
7. The gift was placed inside a beautifully decorated box.
8. For six summers I've vacationed in Québec.
9. What is the name of your favorite book?
10. The dome above our heads looked like the sky.
11. If you sit near me, you may catch my cold.
12. Have you seen the new exhibit at the Art Gallery?
13. They live down the street from us.
14. Put the camera on the table.
15. The boxer fell outside the ring.
16. She waited through the long night at the hospital.
17. Don't go without your briefcase.
18. Phil jumped from the porch onto the grass below.
19. We've lived behind the store for ten years.
20. Everyone except Sue took the test.

The Conjunction

A conjunction is a word or words used to connect sentence parts.

Coordinating Conjunctions. The three conjunctions used only to connect similar sentence parts are *and*, *but*, and *or*. They are called **coordinating conjunctions.**

Correlative Conjunctions. A few conjunctions are used in pairs: *not only . . . but (also); either . . . or; neither . . . nor; both . . . and; whether . . . or.* These conjunctions are called **correlative conjunctions.**

Subordinating Conjunctions. Words used to introduce adverb clauses are called **subordinating conjunctions.** These words not only introduce the subordinate clause but link it to the main clause. Their chief function is to make clear exactly what is the relation between the two clauses. The most common subordinating conjunctions are these:

after	as though	provided	till	whenever
although	because	since	unless	where
as	before	so that	until	while
as if	if	though	when	

Identifying Conjunctions. Underline the conjunctions in the following sentences.

1. I've studied both French and German in School.
2. Sally will be late for the party because she must work till nine.
3. Jim is not only club president, but he is also captain of the football team.
4. It has turned cool, although it's still very sunny.
5. Please tell me if you will be late for dinner.
6. Either Laura or Sue will have the lead in the play.
7. We played tennis until it was too dark to see the ball.
8. Since Mr. Hays does not have Canadian citizenship, he can't vote in the election today.
9. Neither radio nor television offered any good programs last night.
10. After we went to the movie, we stopped for some pizza.
11. Please help us whenever you have the time.
12. I like to play bridge, but I can't keep score.
13. Helen looks as if she's seen a ghost.
14. Dan likes to play tennis and golf.
15. Though he didn't learn to play golf until he was forty, he became a good player.
16. While the teacher passed out the exam questions, Martha gazed out the window.
17. Let us know where you spend the first night of your vacation.
18. Mr. Clark walks as though he is exhausted.
19. Unless they put that coat on sale, I can't afford to buy it.
20. Let's start early in the day before it gets too hot.

Words Used in Different Ways (I)   62

Many words may be used in sentences in different ways:

Noun or Adjective? A word used to name a person, place or thing is a noun. The same word may be used before another noun to tell "what kind." When so used, it is an adjective.

> Mary lives in the *village* of Effingham. (noun)
> Our *village* hall was built in 1930. (adjective)

Pronoun or Adjective? A demonstrative pronoun—*this, that, these,* and *those*—may also be used as an adjective. If the word is used alone in place of a noun, it is a pronoun. If it is used before a noun to tell "which one," it is an adjective.

> *That* is my house. (pronoun)
> *That* house is mine. (adjective)

In a similar way the words *what, which,* and *whose* may be used alone as pronouns or before nouns as adjectives.

> *Which* is your house? (pronoun)
> *Which* house is yours? (adjective)

Determining How Words Are Used. In the following sentences, decide whether the underlined word is used as a noun, a pronoun, or an adjective.

Example: <u>That</u> was a wonderful movie. *pronoun*

1. <u>Whose</u> car shall we take? *adjective*
2. Mr. Barnes installed new <u>kitchen</u> cabinets last week. *noun*
3. Many accidents take place in the <u>kitchen</u>. *noun*
4. <u>Whose</u> dog is that? *adjective*
5. <u>Night</u> games attract a great many people. _____
6. <u>Those</u> cameras will go on sale next week. *pronoun*
7. Tom put his new car in the <u>garage</u>. *noun*
8. <u>This</u> is going to be an awfully hot day. _____
9. Do more accidents happen during the day or during the <u>night</u>? _____
10. <u>What</u> answer did you get for the second problem? _____
11. <u>What</u> did you say to the principal? _____
12. <u>Garage</u> sales are very popular in our neighborhood. *noun*
13. I gave Mr. Carlsen's name as a job <u>reference</u>. _____
14. <u>These</u> are my only good walking shoes. _____
15. <u>Which</u> road leads to the village? *pronoun*
16. <u>What</u> <u>reference</u> books do you keep on your desk? _____
17. <u>Linen</u> is made from flax. *noun*
18. <u>Which</u> is the best road? *pronoun*
19. <u>These</u> old shoes are very comfortable. _____
20. My <u>linen</u> jacket is too wrinkled to wear. *noun*

Words Used in Different Ways (II) 63

Adjective or Adverb? Some words have the same form whether used as adjectives or as adverbs. To tell whether a word is used as an adjective or an adverb, determine what other word in the sentence it goes with, or modifies. If it modifies a noun or a pronoun (telling *what kind*), it is used as an adjective:

> Tom is a *fast* driver. (adjective)

If it modifies a verb (telling *how, when, where,* or *to what extent*), it is used as an adverb:

> Tom always drives *fast*. (adverb)

Adverb or Preposition? A number of words may be used either as prepositions or as adverbs. If the word is followed by a noun or pronoun, it is probably a preposition. The noun or pronoun is its object.

> Your books are *in* the car. (preposition)

If the word in question is not followed by a noun or pronoun, it is probably an adverb.

> Climb *in*. (adverb)

Determining How Words Are Used. In the following sentences, decide whether the underlined word is used as an adjective, an adverb, or a preposition.

Example: We took a <u>slow</u> train out from the city. *adjective*

1. The <u>late</u> movie on television last night was exciting. *adjective*
2. Put your suitcase <u>down</u>. *adverb*
3. The Australian finished <u>first</u> in the race. *adverb*
4. Mrs. Graves arrived <u>late</u> for the board meeting. *adverb*
5. Climb <u>aboard</u>. *adverb*
6. Sarah put her packages <u>inside</u> the car. *preposition*
7. Hal and Jim raced <u>down</u> the hill. *preposition*
8. Wally pulled his belt <u>tightly</u> around him. *adjective*
9. You can look <u>over</u> the edge of the cliff but be careful. *preposition*
10. The <u>first</u> step is to plan our trip. *adverb*
11. I'm so glad to see you at my house; please come <u>inside</u>. *adverb*
12. The Kesslers always go <u>south</u> for the winter. *preposition*
13. He spoke so <u>low</u> that I could hardly hear him. *adjective*
14. The dress is too <u>tight</u> for Mary. *adjective*
15. Can you tell that I've never played tennis <u>before</u>? _____
16. Marge and I have never been <u>close</u> friends. _____
17. I'm afraid I went <u>straight</u> when I should have turned left. _____
18. They've lived in the <u>south</u> part of town for many years. _____
19. <u>Before</u> the show we all went out for pizza. _____
20. Arthur has a <u>low</u> voice. _____

The Infinitive

There are a number of highly useful words in English that are difficult to classify as parts of speech. These are **infinitives, participles,** and **gerunds.** They are called **verbals** because all of them are formed from verbs. Usually, the infinitive is preceded by "to." The kinds of infinitives are as follows:

ACTIVE PRESENT	to give to ask
PASSIVE PRESENT	to be given to be asked
ACTIVE PERFECT	to have given to have asked
PASSIVE PERFECT	to have been given to have been asked

The infinitive may be used as a noun, an adjective, or an adverb.

NOUN	*To see* is to believe.
ADJECTIVE	This is the book *to read*.
ADVERB	We went *to see* the mayor.

Identifying Infinitives. Underline the infinitive in each sentence.

1. She has a hard job to do.

2. To be sympathetic with his problems is sometimes very difficult.

3. We have lots of food to eat.

4. The girls came over to talk with Sally today.

5. Mr. Jordan decided to paint his den this weekend.

6. She taught him to play golf.

7. We intend to visit the museum Sunday.

8. He seems to have given most of his money to charity.

9. To write down your objectives is the first step.

10. Lynn's ambition is to be a lawyer.

11. My parents have gone to St. John's to visit relatives.

12. I have double-checked to be sure of my facts.

13. John listened carefully to get all the directions.

14. To climb in the Rockies has always been my ambition.

15. I am glad to have been asked that question.

16. We are all trying to help the refugees.

17. That is a difficult question to answer.

18. Dorothy plans to attend college next fall.

19. My father likes to play golf on Saturday morning.

20. My sister is planning to be married in June.

The Gerund

The **gerund** is a verbal noun that always ends in *-ing*. It is used in almost every way that a noun can be used.

Seeing is believing. (subject of the verb)
I like *fishing*. (object of the verb)
She is an authority on *gardening*. (object of preposition)

Identifying Gerunds. Find the gerunds in the sentences below. Draw a line under each gerund. Remember to look for the *-ing* ending.

Example: <u>Rising</u> early is hard for me.

1. I don't mind <u>missing</u> breakfast today.
2. <u>Starting</u> early is essential to our plan.
3. Dormitory rules prohibit <u>coming</u> in late.
4. <u>Jogging</u> is Paul's favorite sport.
5. Sally enjoys <u>working</u> with her hands.
6. <u>Managing</u> a motel is his goal.
7. <u>Getting</u> the lead in the play was all Meg thought of.
8. After <u>hiking</u> twenty kilometres, we took a long rest.
9. I like <u>playing</u> the piano.
10. <u>Searching</u> for the lost bracelet took another hour.
11. Mr. Jones teaches <u>creweling</u> to members of the Men's Club.
12. Let's stop <u>worrying</u> about the matter if we can.
13. <u>Getting</u> up early on weekends is not my idea of fun.
14. <u>Practicing</u> judo takes most of Peter's free time.
15. I was given the job of <u>writing</u> the report.
16. Good <u>acting</u> is always a pleasure to see.
17. <u>Driving</u> a car is almost a necessity now.
18. Have you tried <u>resting</u> a bit after dinner?
19. <u>Collecting</u> stamps is Art's favorite hobby.
20. After <u>organizing</u> his notes carefully, he gave an excellent speech.
21. <u>Meeting</u> the prince was exciting for Nancy.
22. <u>Camping</u> in the mountains is Joe's idea of a perfect vacation.
23. I find <u>playing</u> the piano a good way to relax.
24. A short rest now and then will keep you from <u>getting</u> too tired.
25. <u>Reading</u> a good mystery is my idea of a perfect way to spend an afternoon.

The Participle

The **participle** is always used as an adjective to modify a noun or a pronoun. The forms of the participle are these:

PRESENT PARTICIPLE   asking
PAST PARTICIPLE   asked
PERFECT PARTICIPLE   having asked
PASSIVE PERFECT PARTICIPLE   having been asked

Identifying Participles. In each sentence below, underline the participle (or participles). Draw an arrow to the word that the participle modifies.

Example: Sobbing, the little boy looked for his lost toy.

1. Jumping up and down, the cheerleaders led us in the school yell.

2. Having driven a great deal, Peg was not worried by the heavy traffic.

3. Giving me a cross look, the teacher sat down at her desk.

4. The casserole, reheated from last night, will be our dinner tonight.

5. Having been asked to speak at the meeting, Ms. Olson prepared her talk carefully.

6. I saw the old woman sitting on the porch.

7. Exhausted after his long hike, Dave flopped down on the step.

8. The prize, given each year since 1968, will be awarded again this year.

9. Humming aimlessly, the little boy picked up the shells.

10. Mike, having spent all his money on clothes, wasn't able to buy a book at the sale.

11. Holding on to the railing, the old man climbed the stairs slowly.

12. Did you notice the man walking up the hill?

13. We heard the speech given by the professor.

14. My brother, irritated by my question, glared at me.

15. Julia, hearing the footsteps outside the door, looked at me nervously.

16. My cousin, amused by the beginning of the television program, sat back to watch it all.

17. Worried about his finances, Mr. Bennett set up a strict budget.

18. John Diefenbaker, considered one of our greatest Prime Ministers, was born in Grey County, Ontario.

19. Having been asked to dance, Jenny accepted with pleasure.

20. Having been given our directions, we began to work on the project.

Review: The Classification of Words 67

Identifying Parts of Speech. In the following sentences, determine the part of speech of the italicized word. Write the part of speech on the blank after the sentence. Choose from: noun, pronoun, verb, adjective, adverb, preposition, conjunction.

Example: The *gladiolas* were a beautiful shade of yellow. *noun*

1. The grandfather *clock* dates back to the eighteenth century. *noun*
2. The spaghetti sauce *was* too spicy. _____
3. I wish I had *more* spending money. _____
4. Buddy polishes *his* car every weekend. _____
5. It is very hot in the sun, *but* it is pleasant in the shade. _____
6. The pilot was *seriously* injured in the crash. _____
7. *Everyone* should know how to administer first aid. _____
8. I threw my dirty clothes *down* the laundry chute. _____
9. The volunteers in the hospital *distribute* newspapers and mail. _____
10. The van was so *dirty* we couldn't tell what color it was. _____

Identifying Action Verbs and Linking Verbs. In the following sentences, determine whether the italicized verb is an action verb or a linking verb. Mark **A** or **L** on the blank after the sentence.

Example: The road *is* long and winding. *L*

1. I *will be* a camp counselor this summer. _____
2. Dave *has drunk* three cokes with his dinner. _____
3. *Are* you ready for the tournament? _____
4. We *will be driving* to Penticton tomorrow. _____
5. Amy *felt* ill during the practice session. _____

Words Used in Different Ways. In the following sentences, decide how the italicized word is used. Choose from: noun, adverb, preposition, pronoun, adjective.

Example: *This* outline will help me study for the test. *adjective*

1. Do you like *this*? _____
2. I stayed up *until* midnight last night. _____
3. My teachers say that I was a *late* bloomer. _____
4. The toddler lost his balance and fell *down*. _____
5. I was going *down* the stairs when the doorbell rang. _____

What Is a Sentence?

A sentence is a group of words that expresses a complete thought.

INCOMPLETE	The girl in the blue dress. (What about her?)
COMPLETE	The girl in the blue dress smiled shyly.
INCOMPLETE	Tired at the end of a long day. (Who was tired?)
COMPLETE	I was tired at the end of a long day.
INCOMPLETE	Before the game was over. (what happened?)
COMPLETE	Before the game was over, Jim got very tired.

Recognizing Sentences. Read each group of words carefully. If the words form a complete sentence, write **C** in the blank. If the words do not form a complete sentence, write **N** in the blank.

Example: When Mark crossed the street ___*N*___

1. Dolores throwing a ball ___N___
2. Mary Ann prepared the dinner by herself ___C___
3. Ken was startled as the dog leaped at him ___C___
4. At the back of the house ___N___
5. Please be on time for the meeting ___C___
6. Beth's favorite city is Victoria. ___C___
7. Sally, a cheerleader for the last two years ___N___
8. After waving to me, Bob turned the corner ___C___
9. Here comes our train ___C___
10. The coldest February on record ___N___
11. The buffet table was loaded with tempting food ___C___
12. A tall man wearing a brown suit and a big straw hat ___N___
13. Mrs. Olson, who has been a registered nurse for eighteen years ___N___
14. Frightened by the sound of footsteps outside the window ___N___
15. The boys are looking forward to mountain climbing next summer ___C___
16. Moreover, the speaker's main point ___N___
17. Becoming irritated by our questions ___N___
18. Jan Jensen, the pharmacist at the corner drug store ___N___
19. Mrs. Smith drove carefully through the heavy traffic ___C___
20. Mr. Grant works in the garden every day ___C___

Kinds of Sentences

Sentences may be classified according to the purpose of the speaker or writer. The four principal purposes of a sentence are described below.

1. The **declarative sentence** is used to make a statement. The statement may be one of fact, wish, intent, or feeling.

I have seen that movie twice.   I wish I could go on the picnic.

2. The **imperative sentence** is used to state a command, request, or direction. The subject is always You, even though it may not be expressed in the sentence.

(You) Be on time for dinner.   (You) Open the window, please.

3. The **interrogative sentence** is used to ask a question. It is always followed by a question mark.

Do you have a new sweater?

4. An **exclamatory sentence** is used to express strong feeling. It is always followed by an exclamation point.

Don't burn yourself!   How lucky you are!   Keep out!

Classifying Sentences. Read the following sentences and decide the classification of each. Place the number that describes the sentence category in the blank.

Example: Susan is a senior. __1__

1. If only I could go to Newfoundland this summer! __1__
2. Please set the table for lunch. __2__
3. The Prime Minister will visit Egypt next week. __2__
4. Don't you ever get tired of watching television? __1__
5. We bought our car in April, 1980. __2__
6. Didn't I meet you at Banff last summer? __3__
7. Have you ever roasted a turkey? __3__
8. Ouch! I burned my finger! __4__
9. Turn left at the second stop sign. __2__
10. San Marino is the smallest republic in Europe. __1__
11. Initial the top right-hand corner of each sheet of paper. __2__
12. Richard Martin's short stories have appeared in many magazines. __1__
13. Have you ever read *The Chrysalids*? __3__
14. You can't be serious! __4__
15. Meet me at seven o'clock in front of the library. __2__
16. Why are you so worried about the exam? __3__
17. Don't close your mind to the other side of the question. __2__
18. Nancy wants to be a doctor. __1__
19. I can't believe it's all over! __4__
20. Do you attend the concerts given by the Toronto Symphony Orchestra? __3__

Subject and Predicate

The two essential parts of every complete sentence are the subject and the predicate. The **subject** is the person or thing about which something is said. The **predicate** tells something or asks something about the subject.

SUBJECT	PREDICATE
Children	played.
The happy children	played in the sandbox.
Girls	sing.
Both girls	sing in the glee club and chorus.

The Simple Predicate or Verb. In every predicate, the most important word is the **verb.** The simple predicate of the sentence is the verb.

The verb may consist of more than one word: *have sung, might have gone.* When parts of the verb are interrupted by a modifier, the modifier is *not* part of the verb: *were* not *lost, did* not *seem.*

Identifying the Subject and Verb. Underline the verb in each of the following sentences. Draw a circle around each subject. Watch out for modifiers.

Example: Mary cautiously opened the door.

1. Miss Williams is going to New York tomorrow.
2. Your gloves are certainly dirty.
3. Jo Anne's question surprised me.
4. I have never quite made up my mind about the matter.
5. The Martins have played eighteen holes of golf today.
6. The students had never finished their work so quickly before.
7. Mrs. Black has always made her own clothes.
8. The boys will ask the doctor for advice.
9. After his long flight, Tom was very tired.
10. The bridge was never completed.
11. Aunt Helen has just arrived for a week's visit.
12. The old man carefully made his way down the busy street.
13. The witness answered the questions simply and directly.
14. Our team has never beaten yours.
15. The members of our class have just elected officers.
16. Sue has never visited the South.
17. Mr. Gonzales often walks his dog in the evening.
18. The children have been playing outside all day.
19. *Animal Farm* is one of my favorite books.
20. Aunt Marian will prepare Thanksgiving dinner for fourteen people.

Subjects in Unusual Positions

In most sentences, the subject appears before the verb. In many sentences, however, this order is reversed.

Questions. In most questions beginning with interrogative words such as *where, when, why, how, how much,* the subject falls between parts of the verb.

> How does *he* look?   Why is *she* going?   When will *it* begin?
> Where are *they* going?

In questions beginning with *who* or *what,* the verb may follow the subject in normal order.

> Who saw it?   What is going on?

Sentences Beginning with *There* and *Here.* In such sentences, the subject usually follows the verb.

> *There* is the Smiths' house. (house is the subject.)
> *Here* is your jacket. (jacket is the subject.)

Sentences in Inverted Order. For emphasis or variety of style, the subject is sometimes placed after the verb.

> Strolling down the busy street was *Uncle Joe.*
> Behind the house stood the *garage.*

Identifying Subjects and Verbs. Underline the verb in each sentence below. Circle the subject.

> Example: By the road stood an old man

1. What happened to your car?
2. From the Maritimes have come many of our great Canadians.
3. Here are your gloves.
4. What are you doing New Year's Eve?
5. There is the best passer on the team.
6. How much does a cup of coffee cost at that restaurant?
7. At the top of the stairs stood Aunt Martha?
8. From the little girl came a drawn-out sigh.
9. There are many obstacles in our path.
10. When will you be coming to Regina?
11. From the playpen came the cries of my little nephew.
12. Where is Cliff going on his vacation?
13. Driving cautiously down the street was my Uncle Craig.
14. Among the hospital visitors was Mrs. Todd.
15. Where did Helen put the tickets?
16. Walking rapidly toward me was the principal.
17. Here is a picture of Terry Fox.
18. How have you dealt with the problem in the past?
19. Why have you run out of money so fast?
20. Up the ladder climbed the little boy.

The Direct Object

The **direct object** is a word to which the verb carries the action from the subject. Think of the verb as a baseball. If someone or something catches it, the verb has gone directly to its object.

Action verbs with a direct object are called **transitive verbs.**

> I read the *book*. (read what?)
> Our team won the *game*. (won what?)
> Dave has studied *Latin*. (has studied what?)

The direct object tells *what* after the verb. If the word tells *how, when, where,* or *why*, it is an adverb.

> Ann walked *slowly*. (*slowly* tells how; it is an adverb.)

Identifying Direct Objects. Underline the verb or verb phrase in each of the following sentences. Circle the direct object of the verb. Do not include modifiers.

Example: Jane gave a birthday present to Kate.

1. The candidate made many promises during the campaign.

2. I lost my voice before the play.

3. Mother will drive Kim to her swimming lesson.

4. Myra Hayes reviews movies for the local paper.

5. Rhoda has a theory about the robbery.

6. The buffet included three salads.

7. Who hit the ball through Mr. Brown's window?

8. We visited Prince Edward Island during our spring vacation.

9. Dave is taking French this semester.

10. Connie cut the grass last night.

11. Have you dusted the furniture in the living room?

12. Jane has knit three sweaters this winter.

13. The Clarks are having a garage sale Friday.

14. When she tripped on the stairs, Janet hurt her ankle.

15. Have you ever read *Great Expectations* by Charles Dickens?

16. Pam has not made a decision about her job.

17. Have you paid your bills yet?

18. Donna Storms plays tennis very well.

19. Dan has told the truth about last Monday evening.

20. Have you recorded the results of your experiment?

The Indirect Object

The **indirect object** of the verb tells to or for whom, or to or for what, something is done.

> Tell *me* a story.   Show *me* your notebook.

A verb has an indirect object *only* if it also has a direct object. The words *to* and *for* are never placed before an indirect object. When followed by a noun or pronoun, *to* and *for* are always prepositions.

> Helen told *Sue* a joke. (*Sue* is the indirect object.)
> Helen told a joke to *Sue*. (*Sue* is the object of the preposition.)

Identifying Indirect Objects. Underline the indirect object in each of the following sentences. Do not include any direct objects.

> Example: Bill lent <u>Howard</u> his jacket.

1. Lisa told the children a story about an elephant.
2. Give me one good reason for doing that job!
3. Pat gave Dick a record for his birthday.
4. We mailed Barbara a Christmas package.
5. Please tell me your new address.
6. The principal gave Tim a lecture.
7. I'll tell you the truth.
8. Mrs. Barnes gave Chris a reward for finding her briefcase.
9. Please show me the best way to upholster a chair.
10. Norman handed the bellboy a tip.
11. The University Club awarded Joy a scholarship to study marine biology.
12. I wish you great success.
13. Mr. Brent showed Sam his garden.
14. Mrs. Todd promised me a reward for finding her dog.
15. Dr. Jordan gave his church a large contribution.
16. I'll read the twins a story before their bedtime.
17. Grandfather told me a story about his boyhood.
18. I shall give the Salvation Army my used clothing.
19. The company president gave Mom a watch at her retirement party.
20. Mr. Osborn showed his class some photographs taken on his trip.

Predicate Words

The linking verb links its subject to a word in the predicate. The word in the predicate, so linked, is called a *predicate word*. The subject may be linked to a *predicate noun, a predicate pronoun,* or a *predicate adjective.*

> Our math teacher is *Ms. Carson.* (predicate noun)
> That book is *his.* (predicate pronoun)
> Your dress is *pretty.* (predicate adjective)

Identifying Predicate Words. Underline the predicate word in each of the following sentences. Look for the linking verbs to help you find the predicate word.

Example: Selma's editorial was extremely effective.

1. Susan is always very sure of herself.
2. My oldest brother is George.
3. That big black dog is mine.
4. Salespersons in Eaton's are usually very helpful.
5. The speaker of the meeting was a famous scientist.
6. This homemade chili tastes good.
7. Ann feels miserable because of her bad cold.
8. Don't take that book; it's mine.
9. Eli Mandel is my favorite poet.
10. Amy's new dress is blue.
11. I felt cold after watching the football game all afternoon.
12. The Doctor is very modest about her achievements.
13. The Grahams' house is a bungalow.
14. Mr. Beck's cherry pie tasted delicious.
15. It was I who answered the phone.
16. That is the most valuable coin in my collection.
17. Mrs. Brown looked anxious as she picked up the phone.
18. My chemistry teacher is Mr. Harrison.
19. Jeff's room looks messy; it needs a good cleaning.
20. The whole week of our camping trip was rainy.

Compound Parts of Sentences 75

Subjects, objects, and verbs may all be compound. That is, they may include more than one part of the same kind. The parts are joined by a conjunction.

1. **COMPOUND SUBJECT**   Ten *girls* and twelve *boys* made up the kindergarten class.
2. **COMPOUND VERB**   The old car *sputtered* and *shuddered*.
3. **COMPOUND DIRECT OBJECT**   He grows *lettuce* and *tomatoes* in his garden.
4. **COMPOUND INDIRECT OBJECT**   He told *Mary* and *me* a story.
5. **COMPOUND OBJECT OF PREPOSITION**   Mr. Todd wrote a story about *Tom* and *Jim*.
6. **COMPOUND PREDICATE WORD**   Mrs. Elliott looks *thoughtful* and *sad*.
7. **COMPOUND PREDICATE**   I've already *dusted the furniture* and *swept the floors*.

Determining Compound Parts of Sentences. Look at the italicized words in each sentence below. From the list above, decide what kind of compound the words are. Put the corresponding number in the blank.

Example: The girls were *happy* but *subdued*. __6__

1. He keeps busy with *books* and *television* while he's in the hospital. _____
2. Helen received packages from *Ontario* and *Québec* on her birthday.
_____
3. Mr. Bennett ordered three *shirts* and two *ties* from the catalogue.
4. Those girls in the car ahead of us must be *Linda* and *Jane*. _____
5. Sam is exhausted; he *has jogged* and *bicycled* all day. _____
6. I gave *Tom* and *Frank* a piece of my mind. _____
7. The *principal* and the *heads of departments* are attending a conference today. _____
8. Bob plays on the basketball *team* and the football *team*. _____
9. Sally visited *Manitoba* and *Saskatchewan* last summer. _____
10. Dick *studied his history assignment* and *did his math problems* for the next day. _____
11. *Punch* and *The Canadian Geographic* are two of my favorite magazines. _____
12. Miss Thomas questioned *Mark* and *Tim* about their plans for the future. _____
13. *Helen* and *Martha* dreaded the long trip ahead of them. _____
14. The little girls *played hopscotch* and *jumped rope*. _____
15. Please tell *Mother* and *Father* Mr. Spencer's question. _____
16. I bought *milk* and *eggs* at the grocery store. _____
17. The children hunted in vain for their *caps* and *mittens*. _____
18. Mr. McDonald spent all his savings for his *house* and *car*. _____
19. The principal gave *Tim* and *Mike* some sound advice. _____
20. Mrs. Storms *read More Joy in Heaven* and *reviewed it for her club*.
_____

The Prepositional Phrase

A **phrase** is a group of words without a subject and a verb, used as one part of speech. A **verb phrase** is two or more words used as a verb: *might have gone, should have given, could have seen*. A **noun phrase** is two or more words used as a noun: *the Berlin Wall, High Park*.

The **prepositional phrase** consists of the preposition, its object, and modifiers of the object. The object of a preposition is always a noun, a pronoun, or a group of words used as a noun.

The adjective phrase always comes immediately after the noun or pronoun it modifies.

My check *for the dress* is in the mail. (*for the dress* modifies *check*.)

The adverb phrase tells *how, when,* or *where* about a verb, adjective or adverb.

The boy fell *on the stairs*. (*on the stairs* tells *where* he fell.)

Identifying Prepositional Phrases. In the following sentences, underline the prepositional phrase. Circle the word or words that each phrase modifies.

Example: The girl in the yellow dress is my cousin.

1. Jane Austen was born in 1775.

2. My jacket is the one with brass buttons.

3. Bill Carter took five subjects during his sophomore year.

4. The old man stood patiently at the door.

5. I stumbled over Tom's feet.

6. Behind the counter stood the worried clerk.

7. Ms. Kramer is the coach of our debate team.

8. Our team has never played against yours.

9. The tall man across the room is tonight's speaker.

10. The ball was thrown over the roof.

11. Mrs. Garner poured some iced tea into my glass.

12. Dan drove slowly past the corner.

13. The name of the book is *Alone*.

14. Our house is located beyond the city limits.

15. Throughout the night the doctor stayed nearby.

16. Maria fell off the ladder and sprained her ankle.

17. Under the table the dog waited.

18. We are proud because we stayed within our budget.

19. I'll tell you a story about pioneer days.

20. We visited the park between rain showers.

The Infinitive Phrase

The **infinitive phrase** usually begins with the word *to*. The phrase consists of *to*, the infinitive, its complements, and its modifiers.

Carla wants *to be a lawyer*.
(The infinitive phrase is the object of *wants*.)

To win at chess requires much concentration.
(The infinitive phrase is the subject.)

Milo was glad *to be invited to the party*.
(The infinitive phrase modifies the adjective *glad*.)

Identifying Infinitive Phrases. Underline the infinitive phrase in each of the following sentences.

Example: Joe intends <u>to work hard</u>.

1. To be objective in my decision is hard.

2. Does Joan have enough change to make a phone call?

3. Always try to proofread your paper before you turn it in.

4. Ellen is able to swim six lengths of the pool.

5. The Harlow twins came to play with my little brother.

6. Would you like to talk to me?

7. I was happy to give you a ride home.

8. To move to a larger house would be unwise for us now.

9. Fred was frightened to be alone in the old house.

10. Megan is trying to practice the piano an hour a day.

11. To be a doctor is Ann's goal.

12. To be Prime Minister is our member of parliament's ambition.

13. Did you have time to feed the kittens?

14. Mr. and Mrs. Taylor plan to go to Florida this winter.

15. The mayor decided to call a press conference.

16. Dick always tries to do his best.

17. Sarah tried to paint the ceiling of her room.

18. The lecturer was asked to speak for half an hour.

19. Our plan is to go to Vancouver in October.

20. To play tennis every day is Jim's ambition for the summer.

The Participial Phrase

The **participial phrase** is always used as an adjective phrase to modify a noun or pronoun. It includes the participle together with its modifiers, objects, or predicate words.

The present participle form *always* ends in *-ing*, but the endings for past perfect and passive perfect participles may vary.

Walking rapidly, we reached the town in fifteen minutes.

Annoyed by the noise, the teacher spoke sharply to the class.

Tom, *having won the chess game,* looked up happily.

Having won every game but one, John now led the junior division.

Identifying Participial Phrases. Underline the participial phrase. Draw an arrow to the word that the participle modifies.

Example: Mr. Flynn, annoyed by his secretary's question, answered impatiently.

1. Having been on the road for four days, the Todds were exhausted.
2. That hymn, sung by many generations of churchgoers, is my favorite.
3. Climbing slowly, we approached the top of the hill.
4. Surprised by my question, Mrs. Ormond answered slowly.
5. Phil, worn out by his long trip, slept for twelve hours last night.
6. Watching me closely, the dog came toward me.
7. Staring out the window at the rain, Bob became more and more impatient.
8. Having been hurt in the first game, Al sat on the bench for the rest of the season.
9. The plates, brought from Denmark by my grandmother, are on display in the dining room.
10. The cookies, baked this morning, were all gone by five o'clock.
11. Having come out in the cool night air, Mr. Troy looked up at the sky.
12. The children, waiting for the play to begin, grew bored.
13. Working hard all day, the boys finished the job by dinner time.
14. Driven from their homelands, many people each year seek refuge in Canada.
15. Jumping up and down, the cheerleaders urged the team on.
16. The basketball team, encouraged by its performance in the semifinals, went on to the finals.
17. Having recorded the results of the experiment, Kate closed her notebook.
18. We saw an old woman walking up the path.
19. Having been told of her job offer, Kathy smiled happily.
20. Having spent the afternoon at the beach, Alice was hot and tired.

The Gerund Phrase

The **gerund phrase** consists of the gerund, which always ends in *-ing,* and its modifiers and complements. The gerund phrase is *always* used as a noun.

> *Driving a car* takes concentration.
> (The gerund phrase is the subject of the verb *takes*.)

> Paul finished *painting the ceiling.*
> (The gerund phrase is the direct object of *finished.*)

> After *hiking for two hours,* we sat down to rest.
> (The gerund phrase is the object of the preposition *after.*)

Identifying Gerund Phrases. Underline the gerund phrases in the sentences below.

Example: <u>Brisk walking</u> is Don's favorite exercise.

1. Keeping a light on in the house helps discourage robbers.

2. Mrs. Norman enjoys playing bridge.

3. I remember promising Steve my old bike.

4. Standing during a two-hour train trip is not my idea of fun.

5. Do you like sailing on the lake?

6. Volunteering at the hospital is just one of Helen's activities.

7. Mrs. Brent enjoys watching quiz shows on television.

8. Allow twenty minutes a kilogram for roasting the turkey.

9. Taking out the garbage is not my favorite job around the house.

10. Understanding a foreign language and speaking it well are two different things.

11. Acting in high school and college plays helped prepare Tim for Broadway.

12. Collecting stamps is a popular hobby.

13. Rushing through your chores will get you nowhere.

14. Don't you ever get tired of listening to the radio?

15. Mr. Olson never tires of talking about his grandchildren.

16. Bird watching with binoculars is a popular pastime.

17. Arguing with me takes much of my little brother's time.

18. Constant complaining helps no one.

19. Listening to the concerto is sheer pleasure for Joan.

20. After standing behind the counter all day, Jim likes to relax at night.

The Appositive Phrase

An **appositive** is a word placed after another word to explain or identify it. The appositive *always* appears after the word it explains or identifies. It is *always* a noun or pronoun, and the word it explains is *also* a noun or pronoun.

> My uncle, *a lawyer*, is visiting us.
> My teacher, *Ms. Marshall*, is very strict.

An **appositive phrase** consists of the appositive and its modifiers, which may themselves be phrases.

> My radio, *an old portable*, is in the repair shop.
> (The appositive phrase identifies *radio*. The adjective *old* modifies *portable*.)
> The boys climbed the mountain, *one of the highest in the West*.

Identifying Appositive Phrases. Underline the appositive phrase in each of the following sentences.

Example: Our house, a brick bungalow, is on Oak Street.

1. Queen Victoria, one of England's greatest monarchs, ruled for sixty-three years.

2. Jane made the salad, a tossed one with French dressing.

3. Harvey Jensen, the pro at the country club, is giving me golf lessons.

4. James Hilton's book, *Lost Horizon*, has been filmed twice.

5. Chemistry, Sue's favorite subject, is easy for her.

6. Jerry is visiting in Peace River, his old home town.

7. Mr. and Mrs. Miller, our neighbors for the past eight years, are moving to Québec.

8. Have you ever read *The Red Pony*, a novel by John Steinbeck?

9. Groucho Marx the star of many film comedies, also had his own television show.

10. The boys repaired our television set, an eighteen-year-old portable.

11. The poem, one of Robert Frost's best, is called *The Death of the Hired Man*.

12. I can't find my notebook, the one with my history notes in it.

13. Dick's new suit, a gray flannel one, makes him look much older.

14. We enjoy walking, an easy exercise.

15. The theater, an old and drafty one, is nevertheless always crowded.

16. My math teacher, Miss Holmes, has taught for twenty years.

17. The garage, a two-car one, is attached to the house.

18. My sister, a graduate of the University of Calgary is now studying law.

19. Our dog, a cocker spaniel, is ten years old.

20. Mrs. Norbert, the president of the company, will speak at the dinner.

Review: The Parts of a Sentence   81

Determining Grammatical Function. In the following sentences, determine how the italicized word is used. Choose from: subject, predicate, direct object, indirect object, predicate noun, predicate pronoun, predicate adjective.

Example: Chris serves a tennis *ball* with ease. _____*direct object*_____

1. Dad hasn't read that *book* yet. _____

2. I am reading a suspenseful mystery *story*. _____

3. Please pass *me* the salt. _____

4. The hot *weather* has everyone on edge. _____

5. Last winter was the *coldest* on record. _____

6. Randy is too *shy* to go to the party alone. _____

7. I stapled my answer *sheet* to the test. _____

8. The teacher gave *us* a quiz in class this morning. _____

9. It was *she* who won the trophy. _____

10. Many *people* are lonely at Christmas time. _____

Identifying Phrases. In the following sentences, determine the way in which the italicized phrase is used. Choose from: prepositional phrase, infinitive phrase, participial phrase, gerund phrase, appositive phrase.

Example: Our television, *a Zenith*, gets excellent reception. *appositive*

1. Mr. Williams, *the principal of our school*, is a kind man. _____

2. We were sitting *under the tree* when the lightning struck. _____

3. *Cleaning closets* is our annual spring chore. _____

4. Mrs. Moss, *having taught for twenty years*, is a real pro. _____

5. Hector is better at French, *his native language*, than English. ____

6. The auto mechanic will try *to diagnose the problem*. _____

7. *Working diligently on my homework* was important. _____

8. The lamp *in the living room* needs a new bulb. _____

9. All of my friends want *to ride on my motorcycle with me*. _____

10. The tree, *felled by Peter's ax*, toppled with a crash. _____

The Simple Sentence

A **simple sentence** contains only one subject and predicate. Both the subject and predicate may be compound. Compound means having two or more similar parts.

COMPOUND SUBJECT   *Bill* and *Dave* are going fishing tomorrow.
COMPOUND VERB   Joe *swept* and *mopped* all morning.
COMPOUND PREDICATE   Mr. Jordan *carries mail in the daytime* and *clerks in a store in the evening.*

The compound predicate has two verbs having the same subject. At least one of the verbs has a complement.

Identifying Simple Sentences. Underline the compound parts in each of the following sentences. Look for compound subjects, compound verbs, and compound predicates.

Example: Jim and Frank play chess every noon.

1. The children jumped and shouted when they saw Santa Claus.

2. Marie sharpened her pencil and opened her notebook.

3. Fredericton and St. John's are interesting cities.

4. The members of the cast came out and bowed.

5. Mr. Thomas washed the walls and painted the kitchen ceiling.

6. Sally and Frances will leave for the East on Friday.

7. The heat and humidity make it hard to breathe.

8. Paul St. Pierre and Jack London are two of my favorite modern authors.

9. John measured the flour and poured the milk carefully.

10. The children raced home and told their mother the news.

11. Sue and Joan were startled by the sudden clap of thunder.

12. Mrs. Owens has made two dresses and has knit three sweaters this year.

13. Frank went to Mr. Desmond and apologized for his behavior.

14. Marian and Sheila were aware of the problem.

15. Mrs. Gilman stood up and bowed.

16. Both the radio and the television have broken down.

17. The porch and the patio are both cooler than the house.

18. When the war was over, people danced and shouted in the streets.

19. Paul presided at the meeting and did a fine job.

20. Mrs. Todd always waves and smiles as we walk past.

The Compound Sentence

The compound sentence consists of two or more simple sentences put together. The parts are joined by a comma and a coordinating conjunction (such as *and, or, for, nor*), or with a semicolon. Conjunctive adverbs (*then, moreover, hence, consequently,* etc.) are also sometimes used to join parts of a compound sentence. The conjunctive adverb is preceded by a semicolon. In the compound sentence, each verb has a different subject. In the compound predicate, every verb has the same subject.

> Martha has been painting her room, *but* Peg went to the movies.
> Mrs. Miller likes to play bridge, *and* her niece is her favorite partner.
> Sally entered the room cautiously; she had heard footsteps there.
> Our trip took five days; consequently, we are exhausted.

Identifying Compound and Simple Sentences. Decide which of the following sentences are compound and which are simple. Place **S** or **C** in the blank after the sentence.

1. I haven't seen Ann lately, and I won't see her again till fall. _____

2. Mr. Holmes listens to the news every night, and then he goes to bed. _____

3. Helen is going to Spain today and will come home July 25. _____

4. Will you wait for me, or do you want to go ahead? _____

5. The children argue and wrangle over every little thing. _____

6. We had nearly finished our thirty-six holes of golf, and I was exhausted. _____

7. I had originally planned to attend the meeting; however, now I find I can't. _____

8. Mrs. Brent likes to drive; she finds it relaxing. _____

9. Marian is afraid of the water; consequently, she had trouble passing the swimming test. _____

10. They went to the stadium; however, the game had been rained out.

11. Should I carve the roast, or do you want to do it? _____

12. Ellen was calm after the accident, but Jane was very nervous. _____

13. On their vacation, the Smiths golfed and swam every day. _____

14. The Millers and the Ogdens like to attend concerts together. _____

15. I did my grocery shopping today; consequently, our cupboard is full. _____

16. The Prime Minister will hold a press conference today. _____

17. Mr. Nelson looked angry; accordingly, I wasn't eager to introduce myself. _____

18. Shall we have a picnic, or would you like to eat inside? _____

19. Dan showered and dressed in his best clothes. _____

20. The ice cream was partly melted; nevertheless, it tasted good. _____

The Clause

A **clause** is a group of words containing a verb and its subject.
A clause that can stand by itself as a sentence is a **main clause.**

    S.   **V.**   **S.**   **V.**
He walked down the street.   Ken plays in the band.

A clause that cannot stand by itself as a sentence is a **subordinate clause.**

    S.   **V.**
As I approached the house—(What happened?)

    S.   **V.**
If you come to my house—(Then what?)

Phrase or Clause? A clause has a subject and a verb. A phrase does not.

    Losing my amethyst ring was a blow. (phrase)
    When I lost my ring, I was unhappy. (clause)

Identifying Clauses and Phrases. Read each sentence below. If the italicized group of words is a phrase, write **P** in the blank. If it is a clause, write **C.**

    Example: *When I recover from the flu,* I'll leave on my trip. __*C*__

1. *If you have solved that puzzle,* here's a harder one. _____
2. *Walking toward the old house,* Joan met no one. _____
3. The box *which came in the mail today* contains Jack's birthday present. _____
4. Do you know *what is in the box?* _____
5. We saw the old woman *climbing the stairs.* _____
6. *Nodding to me casually,* the principal went into his office. _____
7. *When Amy saw her father,* she rushed up to him. _____
8. We saw the old woman *as she climbed the stairs.* _____
9. *After listening to the teacher's directions,* the class began to take the test. _____
10. This is the record *that I sent for.* _____
11. *Smiling cheerfully,* Kim walked down the hall. _____
12. *If you can spare the time,* let's go to the movie tonight. _____
13. *Striding down the hall,* Mr. Sims looked neither right nor left. _____
14. *When I came home,* I found my brother there ahead of me. _____
15. *Opening the mail,* Mrs. Harris found three bills. _____
16. *After they had fought the cold in January,* the Millers went south in February. _____
17. *If you like Nova Scotia,* you will love Prince Edward Island. _____
18. There goes the ambulance, *hurrying to the hospital.* _____
19. Be quiet *until the buzzer sounds.* _____
20. *Standing in the rain at the parade,* Fred got drenched. _____

The Complex Sentence

The complex sentence consists of one main clause and one or more subordinate clauses. The subordinate clause modifies a word in the main clause.

> *After Dan studies,* he often watches television. (subordinate clause modifies *watches*)
>
> This is the week *when the Todds go on vacation.* (subordinate clause modifies *week*)
>
> *After Ann made the salad,* she set the table. (subordinate clause modifies *set*)

Identifying Simple, Compound, and Complex Sentences. Read the following sentences, and indicate whether each is simple, compound, or complex.

Example: I'm going to bed early because I'm tired. _*complex*_

1. We rang the doorbell, but no one answered it. _____

2. I wrote Jane a letter while she was away at camp. _____

3. Have you seen Mr. Nelson's garden at the back of his house? _____

4. When Miss Jones entered the room, we all became quiet. _____

5. Susan likes chemistry, but she likes physics better. _____

6. Since we've lost every game but one, no one is excited about football this year. _____

7. When I'm tired, I'm not good company for anyone. _____

8. Wandering aimlessly up the path, Mr. Cutter approached the house. _____

9. Susan sang a solo and accompanied herself on the piano. _____

10. When the rain began, we were playing tennis. _____

11. When Uncle Jack comes to town, we all have a good time. _____

12. I worked all morning, and then I relaxed in the afternoon. _____

13. Beth likes all seasons of the year, but she likes fall best. _____

14. On our trip we drove every afternoon until five o'clock. _____

15. Dave began to feel better before the doctor arrived. _____

16. Whistling loudly, Ken walked past the cemetery. _____

17. How many lakes can you see from Lookout Mountain? _____

18. If you want your car really clean, let George wash it. _____

19. I must stay home until the man comes to repair the washing machine. _____

20. Our neighbors are going to the U.S.A. on their vacation, but we will take our vacation at home. _____

The Adjective Clause

An **adjective clause** is a subordinate clause used to modify a noun or pronoun in the main clause. It may be introduced by the pronouns *who, whose, whom, which,* or *that*. These pronouns are called **relative pronouns** because they relate to a noun or pronoun in the sentence. Some adjective clauses begin with an introductory word such as *when* or *where*; occasionally, no introductory word is used.

Is she the girl *whom you met at the party?* (*whom* relates to girl.)
This is a book *that I like.* (*that* relates to *book.*)
This is a house *where Sir Wilfred Laurier slept.* (*where* is an introductory word.)
This is the kind of dessert *I like.* (no introductory word.)

Identifying Adjective Clauses. Underline the adjective clause in each of the following sentences. Circle the word it modifies.

Example: The book *that he wrote* has just been published.

1. Mike, whose ancestors came from Ireland, marched in the St. Patrick's Day parade.

2. The woman who lives next door is a registered nurse.

3. Yellowknife, is a place that I'd like to visit.

4. Math, which is Dave's favorite subject, has always been easy for him.

5. There is the house that I'd like to buy.

6. Larry's letter, which he mailed Tuesday, reached me on Thursday.

7. Summer, which is my favorite season, will be here in another week.

8. Phil is reading *The Call of the Wild*, which is Jack London's most famous book.

9. We live just twenty kilometres from Toronto International Airport, which is Canada's busiest airport.

10. Aurora, Ontario is the town where Barbara was born.

11. I'm taking golf lessons from Erika Laver, who is the pro at the country club.

12. That dog that you found belongs to the Olsons.

13. Is that the jacket you want to buy?

14. There is a chance that Norm will win the election.

15. Is this the letter you were expecting?

16. Over there is the school that I attended.

17. Mr. Hartmann is a history teacher who also coaches track.

18. Is that the antique show you visited?

19. The Harveys have a dog that is fourteen years old.

20. For dinner we had chicken-fried steak, which is my favorite dish.

The Adverb Clause

An **adverb clause** is a subordinate clause used to modify a verb, adjective, or adverb in the main clause. Every adverb clause is introduced by a subordinating conjunction. An adverb clause tells *when, where, why, how, to what extent,* or *how much* about the word it modifies.

ADVERB CLAUSES MODIFYING VERBS

We **left** the bicycle *where we had found it.* (where)
When the rain began, we **were** six kilometres from home. (when)
I **could** hardly **hold** my head up *because I was so sleepy.* (why)

ADVERB CLAUSES MODIFYING ADJECTIVES

Bob is **taller** *than any other boy I know.* (to what extent)
The public library is **bigger** *than it used to be.* (how much)

ADVERB CLAUSES MODIFYING AN ADVERB

Ferguson ran **faster** *than the other track stars did.* (how much)

Identifying Adverb Clauses. Underline the adverb clause in each sentence. Circle the word it modifies.

Example: <u>As we approached the intersection,</u> we (saw) the Nelsons' car.

1. When I delivered the newspaper, I saw Mrs. Simpson at the window.
2. Because that clerk was so helpful, I praised her to the store manager.
3. You may play outside until it's dark.
4. Vince becomes nervous when he speaks in public.
5. Please visit us whenever you are in the Grimsby area.
6. Nero fiddled while Rome burned.
7. You may have piano lessons if you will practice an hour a day.
8. If the jacket is too big for you, I can alter it.
9. Mother took a nap while Amy and I went bicycling.
10. Phone us when you arrive in town.
11. Take a walk until dinner is ready.
12. The movie was just beginning as we bought our tickets.
13. When we arrived in Québec City, we took a taxi to our hotel.
14. Since I'll be late for dinner, I'll get a sandwich downtown.
15. Whenever you make a promise, you must keep it!
16. She can swim better than Bob can.
17. Although I'd never been in the Martins' house before, I felt at home there.
18. Since they left Sarnia, the Smiths have lived in three other cities.
19. When you listen to music on the radio, do you hum along with it?
20. You may have the job if you will work hard at it.

The Noun Clause

A **noun clause** is a subordinate clause used as a noun in the sentence. A noun clause may be used as subject or direct object of the verb, as a predicate noun, as object of the preposition, or as an appositive.

Every direct quotation is a noun clause without an introductory word.

> Mary said, "Dinner is ready." (The noun clause is the object of *said*.)
> Mary said that dinner was ready. (*that* is the introductory word.)

Identifying Noun Clauses. Underline the noun clause in each sentence. If the noun clause is the subject of the sentence, write **s** in the blank. If the noun clause is the direct object, write **D** in the blank.

Example: I know what the answer is. __*D*__

1. Do you know who is the mayor of Kitchener? _____

2. Susan thinks that she will get the job at Martin's Store. _____

3. Whoever phoned us didn't let the phone ring long enough. _____

4. Andy promised that he'd be on time for the party. _____

5. Whether or not she should go camping worried Jane. _____

6. Mr. Sims mentioned that he'd be late for the meeting. _____

7. Whoever sent us this letter should have signed his or her name. _____

8. Who your ancestors were makes no difference to me. _____

9. Mr. Barnes swore that he would tell the truth. _____

10. That anyone else could be doing the same experiments never occurred to him. _____

11. The old man knew where the treasure was kept. _____

12. I'll never forget what happened on our way to the carnival. _____

13. I knew that the safe was behind the picture. _____

14. Amy assured Miss Jordan that she understood the problems. _____

15. What happened on June 30, 1973, will never be forgotten in our town.

16. We knew that we were in for a spell of hot, humid weather. _____

17. Whoever visits us will be assured of a freshly painted room. _____

18. Whoever sent us this Christmas card forgot to sign his name. _____

19. We all believe that Jim will be elected club president.

20. Mr. Norman regrets that he didn't travel more in his youth. _____

Review: Sentence and Clause

Identifying Simple, Compound, and Complex Sentences. Read each of the following sentences carefully and decide if it is a simple sentence, a compound sentence, or a complex sentence. Write the sentence type on the blank.

Example: The typewriter is being overhauled. ___*simple*___

1. The girl who borrowed my sweater left it in her locker. _____
2. I will fold the letters, and Mike will insert them in envelopes. _____
3. After we have finished our work, let's go to the beach. _____
4. Some people in the audience demanded their money back. _____
5. An Irish setter, which is long-haired, sheds a great deal. _____
6. If you need help with your homework, you can call me. _____
7. The ball bounced off the roof and landed in the gutter. _____
8. Either it has gotten chilly out, or there is something wrong with the furnace. _____
9. We aren't allowed to watch television while we are eating. _____
10. Once upon a time, there was a beautiful princess. _____

Identifying Types of Clauses. In the following sentences, determine whether the italicized clause is a noun clause, an adjective clause, or an adverb clause.

Example: The suit *that I bought on sale* is too small. ___*adjective*___

1. Do you remember *what Sandy's telephone number is?* _____
2. Paul became ill *when he was in Moose Jaw*. _____
3. *If I have material left over*, I will make you a shirt. _____
4. *Whoever left the kitchen so messy* had better clean it up. _____
5. Once, *when I was very young*, I ran away from home. _____
6. Lauren, *who is our neighbor*, likes to play in our yard. _____
7. London is a city *where you can leave your heart*. _____
8. *What I just saw* really turned my stomach. _____
9. I told my counselor *that I want to go to college*. _____
10. *Until you are instructed otherwise*, continue with your reading. _____

Identifying Phrases and Clauses. Read each group of words below. If it is a phrase, mark **P** on the blank. If it is a clause, mark **C**.

Example: Driving down the freeway ___*P*___

1. While I was putting on my shoes _____
2. After the heavy rains _____
3. When the rain stopped _____
4. Considering the amount of time _____
5. If I earn enough money doing odd jobs _____

Fragments: Incomplete Thoughts   90

A **sentence fragment** is an incomplete thought that is missing either a subject or a predicate. It is only a part, or fragment, of a sentence.

Father at the end of the day. (Did what? Where is the verb?)
After the movie. (What then? What is the rest of the thought?)

Correcting Fragments Resulting from Incomplete Thoughts. Read the following sentence fragments. Add the words necessary to make each a complete sentence.

1. While walking downtown, the girls _____

   _____

2. At four o'clock _____

   _____

3. In January, our coldest month _____

   _____

4. The delay in shipment _____

   _____

5. On Oak Street _____

   _____

6. When I crossed the street _____

   _____

7. As Susan unwrapped her gift _____

   _____

8. Since Mother hurried down to the sale _____

   _____

9. Nothing on the grocer's shelves _____

   _____

10. The school in our neighborhood _____

    _____

11. Miss Jones, the head librarian _____

    _____

12. Walking through the crowded halls at school _____

    _____

13. If you promise _____

    _____

14. Closing the door quietly _____

    _____

Fragments: Faulty Punctuation

The first word of a sentence begins with a capital letter, and the sentence is closed by a punctuation mark: period, question mark, or exclamation mark. When the writer inserts a period and capital letter too soon, the result is called a **period fault.**

FRAGMENT   While she was reading. She fell asleep.
SENTENCE   While she was reading, she fell asleep.
FRAGMENT   The members stood up. When the Queen entered the House.
SENTENCE   The members stood up when the Queen entered the House.

Correcting Fragments Resulting from Incorrect Punctuation. Find the fragments in each of the following groups of words. Correctly rewrite each by either changing the punctuation or adding the words needed to make a complete sentence.

1. After we went to the movie. We stopped for sundaes. _____

_____

2. Susan's new red dress. Was just right for the occasion. _____

_____

3. Since we had eaten such a big lunch. A light supper. _____

_____

4. Whenever my father watches football. He cheers for the Blue Bombers. _____

_____

5. After our car was washed. It looked much better. _____

_____

6. Our team has won the championship. Twice in the last three years.

_____

_____

7. Although Dad works hard. He always takes time to relax. _____

_____

8. Crossing the street. I stumbled and fell. _____

_____

9. After Sam returned from his canoe trip. He sold his canoe. _____

_____

10. Unless you are sure of the answer. A blank space. _____

_____

Phrases as Fragments

A phrase is a group of words that does not contain a verb and its subject. Therefore, a phrase cannot be a complete sentence by itself. It can only be part of a sentence. A prepositional phrase is usually easy to spot.

FRAGMENT   In their driveway. Stands a brand new station wagon.
SENTENCE   In their driveway stands a brand new station wagon.

A verbal phrase may be harder to spot as a fragment, especially verbals that end in -ing. No word ending in -ing can be a verb unless it is a one-syllable word like sing, ring, or bring. If an -ing word is preceded by is, are, or some other form of be, the two words together are a verb.

PARTICIPLE   looking, running   COMPLETE VERB   is looking, was running

Do not mistake a long infinitive phrase for a sentence. The infinitive phrase does not have a subject.

INCORRECT   My suit is at the dry cleaner's. To be pressed.
CORRECT   My suit is at the dry cleaner's to be pressed.

An appositive phrase may seem like a sentence, but it always lacks a verb.

APPOSITIVE FRAGMENT   Her new dress, made of Irish linen.
SENTENCE   Her new dress was made of Irish linen.

Completing Fragments. Rewrite each group of words to form a complete sentence.

1. Running down the street. _____

_____

2. I know the best thing to do. To present our case before the landlord.

_____

3. We went to the hardware store. To buy some nails. _____

_____

4. Sally found her necklace. In the desk drawer. _____

_____

5. Our dog, a ten-year-old cocker spaniel. _____

_____

6. John, cutting the grass in the front yard. _____

_____

7. Reading quietly. Mother didn't hear us come in. _____

_____

8. That book on how to grow plants indoors. _____

_____

Clauses as Fragments

A subordinate clause cannot stand by itself as a sentence. A sentence may be changed into a subordinate clause by having a subordinating conjunction placed before it.

SENTENCE   The dentist began drilling.
SUBORDINATE CLAUSE   Until the dentist began drilling . . .

Writers sometimes mistakenly place a period before or after a subordinate clause as though it were a sentence.

INCORRECT   John was late. Because his car wouldn't start.
CORRECT   John was late because his car wouldn't start.

Eliminating Fragments. Rewrite each of the following word groups to form a complete sentence.

Example: While hurrying across the street. Mrs. Olson stumbled. *While hurrying across the street, Mrs. Olson stumbled.*

1. While Margaret hunted for her lost glove. _____

_____

2. I'm exhausted. Because I've been hiking for three days. _____

_____

3. My father. After he drove home in a new car. _____

_____

4. Since Kathy has a new job. _____

_____

5. Before we move south. _____

_____

6. Julie was elected. Although she's new in school. _____

_____

7. When he was driving home. _____

_____

8. After we won first place in the province. _____

_____

9. Unless you would rather wait till spring. _____

_____

10. The audience applauded. When the speaker finished her address. _____

_____

Avoiding Run-on Sentences (I)   94

A run-on sentence is two or more sentences written as one sentence. The writer has failed to use an end mark, such as a period, at the end of each sentence.

RUN-ON   Bill broke his arm it has given him a lot of trouble.
CORRECT   Bill broke his arm. It has given him a lot of trouble.

Most run-on sentences are the result of a **comma fault.** A comma is used to join two or more sentences together when each sentence should really stand alone.

COMMA FAULT   Cynthia has a new dress, it is blue and white.
CORRECT   Cynthia has a new dress. It is blue and white.

How To Avoid the Run-on Sentence. If two or more subjects are closely related, it is usually a good idea to join them in one sentence. There are three ways to join sentences correctly:

1. with a comma and a coordinating conjunction:
   This summer I can work at the hardware store, or I can be a lifeguard.
2. with a semicolon:
   Donna has decided which job to take; she will work in the bank.
3. with a semicolon and a conjunctive adverb:
   We ate a big lunch; nevertheless, we were hungry again by six o'clock.

Correcting Run-on Sentences. Put the necessary punctuation in these sentences.

Example: Mark took chemistry this year; he'll take physics next year.

1. Mother went to the antique show, she bought a handsome rocking chair.
2. We won't go on vacation till August we're ready to go right now!
3. Come over to our house, we'd like to see you.
4. Sarah missed her bus, consequently, she was late for work.
5. It's been a cold spring, hence, we've been slow in putting in our garden.
6. We saw the exhibit at the art gallery then we stopped at Nancy's house.
7. No one even looked up when Mr. Ruiz approached we were all doing our math.
8. I didn't study last night, the lights went out during the storm.
9. I like Irving Layton's *The Swimmer*, it's my favorite poem.
10. The Millers live on Elm Street, they've lived there twelve years.
11. Ralph studies hard he's trying to win a scholarship for next year.
12. We'll be on the West Coast in June, however, we won't get to Manitoba.
13. The Smiths spent three weeks in Regina last summer, consequently, they feel as if they know that city pretty well.
14. Ms. Bennett has studied Latin for four years, furthermore, she's had two years of Greek.

Avoiding Run-on Sentences (II)

Correcting Run-on Sentences. Put the necessary punctuation in these sentences.

Example: Our dog is lost;he's been gone for two days.

1. I looked up *endocrinology* in the dictionary, then I looked it up in the encyclopedia.

2. You tell me your ambition, then I'll tell you mine.

3. Don has missed a week of school because of his illness, furthermore, he still doesn't feel well.

4. You cook the dinner I'll do the dishes.

5. Mark is a senior now he's been in debating club for the past two years.

6. Peg has a beautiful voice she'll sing a solo in the Christmas concert.

7. Mrs. Clark has been to Europe four times, moreover she's also been to Japan.

8. Mrs. Means likes to knit she's made four sweaters this year.

9. I'd like to go to Italy, all my ancestors came from there.

10. Ross's savings are almost down to zero, furthermore, there's very little in his checking account.

11. People always remember my birthday it's April Fool's Day!

12. The Sewells would like to go to Europe next summer, however, they don't have enough vacation time.

13. This year Don is working at the drug store, last year he worked at the grocery.

14. The lecturer knew a great deal about his subject, however, his speech was above the heads of most in the audience.

15. Sam drove his brother home then he went back to the meeting.

16. Mrs. Owens has read most of the books in our public library, furthermore, she has over 300 books of her own.

17. Miss Tilden knows hundreds of people by name nevertheless, she has few real friends.

18. Let me know when your meeting is over, then I'll come and pick you up.

19. We had quite a storm last night, there was lots of thunder and lightning.

20. In high school forty years ago Mr. Stillwell learned to type, that knowledge has always been useful to him.

Review: Complete Sentences

Distinguishing Fragments from Complete Sentences. Read each group of words below carefully. All are punctuated as sentences, but some are really fragments. After each fragment, write an **F** on the blank. After each sentence, write an **S** on the blank.

Example: Thinking he was finished with his work. ___*F*___

1. The people who are moving in across the street. _____
2. Directly overhead, a helicopter hovered. _____
3. Climbing into bed and falling asleep. _____
4. Someone is calling for help. _____
5. Were stacked neatly in the linen closet. _____

Rewriting Sentences. All of the items below need revision. Some contain fragments and need to be rewritten as one complete sentence. Others are run-on sentences and need to be rewritten as two sentences or punctuated properly as one sentence.

Example: I spilled something on my shirt. While eating my breakfast.
While eating my breakfast, I spilled something on my shirt.

1. The day will be a real scorcher, the weatherman predicts 30°C.

   _____

2. Forgetting all about his medicine. Dad went off to play golf. _____

   _____

3. If you think you can solve this problem. _____

   _____

4. Grandma left me an inheritance, I can't use it until I'm twenty-one.

   _____

5. Unless you are here by noon. I will leave without you. _____

   _____

6. Today is only Thursday I really wish it were Friday. _____

   _____

7. Even though we were exhausted from the hike. _____

   _____

8. We looked everywhere for the keys. Even under the furniture. _____

   _____

9. My veal was delicious, Dad's lamb chop was not as good. _____

   _____

10. Sometimes, when I am in a very bad mood. _____

    _____

Agreement in Number (I)

There are two numbers in grammar: **singular** and **plural.** A word is singular in number if it refers to one person or thing. A word is plural if it refers to more than one person or thing.

Except for *be,* English verbs show a difference between singular and plural only in the third person and only in the present tense. The third person singular present form ends in *s.*

I, you, we, they **talk**   he, she, it **talks**

The second person pronoun *you* is always used with the plural form of the verb: *you are, you were.* The difference between singular and plural forms of *be* is shown in the past tense as well as the present tense.

PRESENT		PAST	
SINGULAR	PLURAL	SINGULAR	PLURAL
I *am*	we *are*	I *was*	we *were*
you *are*	you *are*	you *were*	you *were*
he, she, it *is*	they *are*	he, she, it *was*	they *were*

Choosing the Correct Verb Form. Underline the correct form of the verb in each sentence below.

1. (Was, Were) you at the meeting last night?
2. We (was, were) walking down the street when I stumbled.
3. (Is, Are) *Little Women* your sister's favorite book?
4. As the dentist (was, were) drilling, I tried to think of pleasant things.
5. (Is, Are) your team ahead of mine in the conference?
6. Sarah (commutes, commute) to her job in the city.
7. (Was, Were) you playing tennis with Joe last night?
8. The concert (was, were) too long to hold my interest.
9. Where (was, were) they going when we saw them last night?
10. How fast (was, were) they going at the time of the accident?
11. (Wasn't, Weren't) the twins good in the play?
12. The Olsons (is, are) going to Vermont next week.
13. They (was, were) not amused by the comedian.
14. They (was, were) out of town when the house burned.
15. (Has, Have) the Nelsons bought a new car?
16. The Millers (was, were) happy about the outcome of the election.
17. You (was, were) up early this morning.
18. How (does, do) Art manage to do so much in one day?
19. (Was, Were) you at the class reunion?
20. The Hefkes (was, were) sitting on their patio when we called.

Agreement in Number (II)   98

The verb agrees only with its subject. Occasionally a word with a different number from that of the subject occurs between the subject and the verb. This word or group of words does not change the number of the verb even though it is closer to the verb than the subject is.

> One of the boys has gone camping. (*one* is the subject.)
> The ball, thrown by the boys, has gone through the Browns' window.
>   (*ball* is the subject.)

The words *with, together with, along with, as well as* are prepositions. The objects of these prepositions have no effect upon the number of the verb.

> The teacher, along with the students, has gone out for fire drill. (*teacher* is the subject.)
> My aunt, along with my cousins, is visiting us. (*aunt* is the subject.)

Choosing the Correct Verb Form. Underline the correct form of the verb in each sentence below.

1. The members of the band (has, have) arrived for practice.
2. The price of houses (keeps, keep) increasing every year.
3. The twins, along with their mother, (is, are) going to the exhibit.
4. One of the women (is, are) planning to give a karate demonstration.
5. (Has, Have) the pair of earrings been found?
6. The sale of shirts (has, have) been scheduled for next Monday.
7. Tom, together with three friends, (is, are) going camping next week.
8. The directors of the bank (is, are) meeting at ten o'clock.
9. One of the best books (tells, tell) about the Inuit.
10. The library, with its thousands of books, (is, are) free to all.
11. Ms. Taylor, along with the other teachers, (is, are) attending a convention.
12. The chairman of the board, together with the directors, (is, are) now coming into the room.
13. The girls in the glee club (was, were) planning a concert.
14. My cousin, along with her friends, (is, are) planning to be in Ottawa next week.
15. Mrs. Thomas, together with other members of the club, (is, are) planning a golf tournament.
16. The seats in the first-grade classroom (was, were) very small.
17. Delivery of the groceries (is, are) being made today.
18. Susan, as well as her neighbors, (is, are) planning a garage sale.
19. The package of Christmas presents (has, have) not arrived yet.
20. My order for the oranges (was, were) placed last week.

Indefinite Pronouns

Some indefinite pronouns are always singular. Others are always plural. *Some, none, all, any,* and *most* are singular when they refer to a quantity. They are plural when they refer to a number of individual items.

SINGULAR			PLURAL	SINGULAR OR PLURAL	
each	someone	nobody	several	some	any
either	everyone	somebody	few	none	most
neither	anyone	everybody	both	all	
one	no one		many		

One of the books *was* lost.
Several in the club *are* good at speaking in public.
Some of the money *was* missing.
Some of the windows *are* dirty.

Choosing the Correct Verb Form. Underline the correct form of the verb in each sentence below.

Example: Somebody (<u>is</u>, are) at the door.

1. Most of the library books (has, have) been returned.

2. Everybody on the bus (was, were) going to Niagara.

3. Few of the men (is, are) going to play in the tournament.

4. Neither of the two cabinet ministers (has, have) explained the matter.

5. All of us (is, are) hoping that Steve will win.

6. Nobody (knows, know) the answer to your question.

7. Several of the retired men (has, have) started volunteer tutoring at the school.

8. One of them (is, are) badly mistaken.

9. Everyone at the birthday party (was, were) somehow related to Jean.

10. No one (is, are) doing his best work.

11. (Is, Are) there any of the pie left?

12. Both of the girls (is, are) going to Carlton College next fall.

13. Many of the club members (wants, want) to visit the Art Gallery.

14. (Is, Are) somebody looking for a lost glove?

15. Some of the salad (has, have) been eaten.

16. Some of us (has, have) never ridden bicycles before.

17. None of the milk (was, were) sour.

18. Each of us (was, were) planning a trip.

19. (Has, Have) anyone seen my sweater?

20. Both of the girls (is, are) good singers.

Compound Subjects 100

Compound subjects joined by *and* are plural.

> Tom and Jim *are* brothers.

Singular words joined by *or, nor, either-or, neither-nor* are singular.

> Neither Barbara nor Kim *is* in the glee club.
> Either Tim or Peter *is* planning to attend the class.
> *Was* roast beef or baked ham on the menu?

When a singular word and plural word are joined by *or* or *nor*, the verb agrees with the subject nearer to it.

> Neither Ann nor her friends *are* coming.
> Either the veterinarian or her assistants *give* the shots.

Choosing the Correct Verb Form with Compound Subjects. In each of the following sentences, underline the correct form of the verb.

Example: Alice and Mary (plans, <u>plan</u>) to attend the same college.

1. Neither the pie nor the tarts (was, were) on Megan's diet.

2. Alice or her mother (is, are) going to collect for the Red Cross this week.

3. Helen and Amy (hopes, hope) to become lawyers.

4. The author's first two novels and last short story (is, are) often quoted.

5. Either my aunt or my uncle (is, are) driving me to camp today.

6. Neither a hot dog nor a hamburger (appeals, appeal) to me today.

7. A steak and a baked potato (is, are) what John likes for dinner.

8. Either Monday or Tuesday (promises, promise) to be a fine day.

9. Guelph and Kitchener (is, are) two of my favorite cities.

10. Neither Miss Brown nor her secretary (is, are) here today.

11. The train and the bus (arrives, arrive) in town at two o'clock.

12. French and German (is, are) spoken in that part of Switzerland.

13. Neither Tom nor Joe (blames, blame) the old man.

14. Either Farley Mowat or Pierre Berton (is, are) my favorite writer.

15. Neither Mrs. Black nor the other club members (is, are) willing to take the responsibility.

16. The debaters and their coach (is, are) awaiting the decision.

17. Neither the silverware nor the dishes (has, have) been washed.

18. The boy's cap and mittens (has, have) been lost.

19. Neither the secretaries nor their boss (plans, plan) to read the correspondence again.

20. Either George or Bill (drives, drive) to the city each day.

Subject Following Verb 101

When the subject follows the verb, you must think ahead to the subject to decide whether the verb is to be singular or plural.

This problem arises in sentences beginning with *There* and *Here*. It also arises in questions beginning with *Who, Why, Where, What,* and *How.*

INCORRECT	Here's the records.
CORRECT	Here *are* the records.
INCORRECT	There's my brothers now.
CORRECT	There *are* my brothers now.
INCORRECT	Who's the women at the window?
CORRECT	Who *are* the women at the window?
INCORRECT	What's the solutions?
CORRECT	What *are* the solutions?

Choosing the Correct Verb Form. Underline the correct form of the verb in each sentence below.

Example: (What's, <u>What are</u>) the problems?

1. (Here's, Here are) the apples you ordered.
2. (Who's, Who are) your bosses at the plant?
3. (What's, What are) your suggestions?
4. In the car (was, were) Helen and her brother.
5. (There's, There are) four people who have been elected to office.
6. (Here's, Here are) the sweet rolls you wanted.
7. (How's, How are) all your tropical fish?
8. (Why's, Why are) all the students late today?
9. (There's, There are) milk and cake on the table.
10. (Who's, Who are) the boys on the track team?
11. Near the highway (was, were) an old house and a barn.
12. Behind the counter (stands, stand) the clerk and the store manager.
13. (What's, What are) the jokes you were going to tell me?
14. (Why's, Why are) his songs always so sad?
15. (Here's, Here are) the fried chicken and salad you ordered.
16. In front of us (was, were) the three little boys.
17. (Here's, Here are) the shoes you left by the door.
18. Outside the door (barks, bark) the three dogs.
19. (What's, What are) your reasons for making that statement?
20. (What's, What are) your answers to those questions?

Using *Don't* and *Doesn't*

The word *does* and the contraction *doesn't* are used with singular nouns and with the pronouns *he, she,* and *it.* The word *do* and the contraction *don't* are used with plural nouns and with the pronouns *I, we, you,* and *they.*

DOES, DOESN'T	DO, DON'T
our friend does	our friends do
he doesn't	we don't
she doesn't	you don't
it doesn't	they don't

Using *Does* and *Don't* Correctly. Underline the correct word in each sentence below.

1. Amy (doesn't, don't) like to play golf.

2. The airplane (doesn't, don't) have any available seats.

3. Why (doesn't, don't) Peggy have her hair cut?

4. The rug (doesn't, don't) cover all the floor.

5. Our dog (doesn't, don't) know any tricks.

6. (Doesn't, Don't) Bill know the answer to this problem?

7. Mr. Ogden likes to play golf, but Mr. Wright (doesn't, don't).

8. Helen (doesn't, don't) make friends easily.

9. Why (doesn't, don't) Dave come over for dinner?

10. The menu (doesn't, don't) include baked ham.

11. The boy in the red shirt and blue jeans (doesn't, don't) look old enough to drive.

12. Onions (doesn't, don't) agree with me.

13. The photograph of Mr. and Mrs. Smith (doesn't, don't) even look like them.

14. That store (doesn't, don't) even sell rugs.

15. Our debate with the Thornwood team (doesn't, don't) begin till ten o'clock.

16. The Prime Minister and his cabinet members (doesn't, don't) meet till tomorrow.

17. Why (doesn't, don't) Dan ring the bell?

18. The director, along with the members of the band, (doesn't, don't) report for rehearsals till tomorrow.

19. That potato salad (doesn't, don't) taste good.

20. (Doesn't, Don't) the superintendent of schools live near you?

Other Agreement Problems (I)   103

Collective Nouns. A collective noun names a group of people or things: *band, jury, crew, group, team*. When a writer refers to a group acting together as one unit, the collective noun is used with a singular verb. When the writer refers to the individuals in the group acting separately, the collective noun is used with a plural verb.

> Our band *is* the best in the country. (united action)
> Our band *were* wearing their new uniforms. (separate actions)

Nouns Plural in Form. Some nouns are plural in form but are singular in meaning: *news, mumps, measles*. There are many words ending in *-ics* that may be singular or plural: *politics, athletics, economics*. These words are singular when used to refer to a subject or a practice.

> Athletics is the department headed by Mr. Smith. (singular)
> His favorite athletics are track and golf. (plural)

Choosing the Correct Verb Form. Underline the correct form of the verb in each sentence below.

> Example: The news of the day (is, are) the subject of Mrs. Martin's commentary.

1. The team (was, were) all grinning after their victory.
2. The jury (has, have) reached a verdict.
3. Measles (is, are) a disease Mr. Smith avoided until he was thirty.
4. The company (was, were) started in 1968 and immediately elected its directors.
5. (Is, Are) mumps prevalent in your town now?
6. Economics (is, are) the science of the production of wealth.
7. The audience (is, are) taking their seats now.
8. Our class (is, are) posing for their yearbook pictures today.
9. Civics (is, are) a study of the rights and duties of citizens.
10. The member's politics (is, are) sometimes questioned by his constituents.
11. The committee (is, are) taking their places around the conference table.
12. The news on the front page (was, were) all bad today.
13. The contents of the briefcase (was, were) a notebook, a newspaper, and a chess set.
14. Economics (is, are) taught in the senior year.
15. Mr. Brown's ethics (was, were) seriously questioned.
16. The old couple (is, are) living on Elm Street.
17. Politics (is, are) the practice of managing affairs of public policy.
18. Canada (is, are) sending a delegate to the conference.
19. The West Indies (is, are) a part of the world I'd like to visit.
20. Economics (was, were) Vicky's major in college.

Other Agreement Problems (II) 104

Titles and Groups of Words. Any group of words referring to a single thing or thought is used with a singular verb. The title of a book, play, film, musical composition, or other work of art refers to one thing, and is used with a singular verb.

> *Saints and Strangers* was written by George Willison.
> The Netherlands is small but prosperous.

Words of Amount and Time. Words or phrases that express periods of time, fractions, weights, measures, and amounts of money are usually singular.

> Fifty dollars *is* too much to charge.
> Half of the book *is* well written.

If a prepositional phrase separates the subject from the verb, the verb is singular if its subject is considered a single thing or thought. The verb is plural if its subject is considered plural.

> Five kilograms of flour was what I ordered.
> Five bags of mail *were* delivered.

Choosing the Correct Verb Form. Underline the correct form of the verb in each sentence below.

1. Half of the province (is, are) mountainous.
2. What we want (is, are) support from the community.
3. *The Rest of the Robots* (was, were) written by Isaac Asimov.
4. Two days (is, are) not long enough for our trip.
5. Three-fourths of his time (is, are) devoted to writing.
6. The Union of Soviet Socialist Republics (is, are) another name for Russia.
7. Eighty-nine cents (is, are) too much to pay for a cantaloupe.
8. "The gods help them that help themselves" (was, were) said by Aesop.
9. Two kilograms of potatoes (is, are) too much for the potato salad.
10. Two weeks (is, are) too little to spend on the vacation we plan.
11. 473.6 mL of sugar (was, were) called for in the recipe.
12. Manitoba (is, are) one of my favorite provinces.
13. Half of our vacation (is, are) over.
14. Three kilograms of coffee (is, are) what Mrs. Means bought today.
15. Anne Murray (is, are) a popular Canadian performer.
16. Fifty cents (is, are) far too much to pay for a cup of coffee!
17. *Fathers and Sons* (is, are) the book I'm reviewing for our club.
18. Three metres of material (was, were) ordered by Mrs. Jordan.
19. "Strangers in the Night" (is, are) a song I like.
20. "It takes a great person to make a good listener" (is, are) what Arthur Helps said.

Relative Pronouns

A relative pronoun agrees with its antecedent in the sentence. If the antecedent is singular, the relative pronoun is singular. If that antecedent is plural, the pronoun is plural. Usually, the meaning of the sentence shows you which word is the antecedent.

Bob is the *boy* who *has* received the promotion. (singular)
They are the *women* who *teach* at West School. (plural)
Libby is the only *one* of the girls who *plays* the piano. (singular)
The Morgans are the sort of *neighbors* who *are* interested in your welfare. (plural)

Choosing the Correct Form of the Verb. In each of the following sentences, underline the correct form of the verb to be used with the relative pronoun.

1. Jim is the football player who (was, were) elected captain of the team.

2. These are the children who (is, are) in the nursery school.

3. Ms. Thornton is one of the women who (is, are) being considered for the church choir.

4. That is one of the articles that usually (appears, appear) on the back page of the paper.

5. There are two men in our town who (has, have) been elected to provincial office.

6. Bob is the boy who (has, have) won the scholarship.

7. Art is a person who (is, are) always ready to help others.

8. I sorted out the stamps that (is, are) worth saving.

9. Alice is the only one of my friends who (has, have) been to Europe.

10. This is the only one of the plants that (grows, grow) well in the shade.

11. Bill is one of the boys who (is, are) out for track.

12. Peter is the only one of my cousins who (lives, live) on the family farm.

13. Mrs. White is the only one who (was, were) not home.

14. That television program is the only one that (interests, interest) me.

15. Mrs. Owen is a woman who always (seems, seem) nervous.

16. Kate is the only one of the students who (has, have) been concerned about the results of the exam.

17. That is the oldest ship in the fleet that (is, are) still in action.

18. The package that we ordered (has, have) just arrived.

19. This is one of the clubs that (has, have) been in existence a long time.

20. Those are the women who (is, are) making a quilt for the church bazaar.

Review: Agreement of Subject and Verb 106

Choosing the Correct Verb Form. Underline the correct form of the verb in each sentence below.

Example: The boy's books (is, <u>are</u>) in his locker.

1. All of the traffic lights at the intersection (was, were) broken.

2. *Humpty Dumpty* and *Old King Cole* (is, are) nursery rhymes.

3. They (was, were) surprised to find their basement flooded.

4. Four of the teachers at our school (is, are) retiring this year.

5. The pencils in the box (was, were) sharpened for the test.

6. The points on several of them (is, are) now dull.

7. The pictures Gabe drew in nursery school (is, are) on the refrigerator door.

8. Each of the lifeguards on the beach (is, are) a good swimmer.

9. My morning chores (take, takes) me hours to finish.

10. The papers from the garbage can (was, were) blowing in the breeze.

11. Two of my teeth (need, needs) filling.

12. All of the shades in the house (has, have) been drawn.

13. Every one of the secretaries (type, types) faster than I.

14. Neither Emily nor Adam (is, are) coming to the meeting.

15. The doorbell and the telephone always (ring, rings) at the same time.

16. Either a hot dog or a hamburger (sound, sounds) good to me.

17. (Here's, Here are) the strawberries for dessert.

18. Behind the garage (was, were) the tallest weeds I have ever seen.

19. Why (is, are) the newspapers stacked up on the porch?

20. The pictures in the album (don't, doesn't) have dates on them.

21. It (doesn't, don't) make sense to drive all the way to Florida.

22. (Don't, Doesn't) anyone in your class live near you?

23. The lawyer's ethics (is, are) not to be questioned.

24. Half of the pie (is, are) gone.

25. Howard is the neighbor who (like, likes) to play football with us.

The Pronoun as Subject

The nominative form of the pronoun is used as the subject of a verb. The problem of which pronoun form to use as subject arises chiefly when the subject is compound. To decide which pronoun form to use in a compound subject, *try each part of the subject by itself with the verb.*

> Mary and (I, me) went to the game. (Mary went; I went, *not* me went)
> The Wilsons and (we, us) gave a party. (The Wilsons gave; we gave,
> *not* us gave)

The Predicate Pronoun. The verb *be* is a linking verb. It links the noun, pronoun, or adjective following it to the subject. A pronoun so linked is called a **predicate pronoun.**

The nominative pronoun form is used as a predicate pronoun.

The problem of which form to use in a predicate pronoun occurs primarily after the verb *be.*

> It was *I* who spoke to you.
> It could have been *they* we saw last night.

Choosing the Correct Pronoun. Underline the correct pronoun in each sentence below:

> Example: The Johnsons and (we, us) are going to the movie.

1. Tom is sure that the winner will be (he, him).
2. Fred and (I, me) cooked the breakfast.
3. It was (he, him) who answered the phone.
4. Yesterday David and (he, him) looked for summer jobs.
5. It could have been (they, them) who telephoned.
6. The Clarks and (they, them) toured the West together last year.
7. Sally and (she, her) played a duet in the piano recital.
8. It is (she, her) who is to blame for the accident.
9. It could have been (he, him) who intercepted the message.
10. The Blacks and (we, us) had dinner together last night.
11. It was (we, us) you heard on the porch last night.
12. Nancy and (I, me) played tennis yesterday.
13. It must have been (she, her) who rang the doorbell.
14. Peter and (he, him) belong to the debate club.
15. It is (we, us) who sent the letter.
16. We and (they, them) plan a camping vacation this summer.
17. Bob and (I, me) plan to go to college in the fall.
18. Sarah and (she, her) are good friends.
19. That could be (he, him) at the door now.
20. Was it (they, them) you saw at the game?

The Pronoun as Object (I)

The objective pronoun form is used as the direct or indirect object. The problem of which pronoun form to use as object of the verb arises chiefly when the object is compound. To decide which pronoun to use with a compound object, *try each part of the object by itself with the verb.*

DIRECT OBJECT   My question irritated Mr. Jones and (he, him).
  (irritated Mr. Jones; irritated him, *not* he)

INDIRECT OBJECT   Ask Betsy and (I, me) your question.
  (ask Betsy; ask me, *not* ask I)

Choosing the Correct Pronoun. Underline the correct pronoun in each sentence.

Example: Tell Jane and (I, <u>me</u>) your birthdate.

1. Please tell Jim and (I, me) if you will be late for the meeting.

2. Ask Don and (she, her) all your questions.

3. Give your brother and (I, me) an honest answer.

4. The mayor presented the senator and (he, him) keys to the city.

5. Don't tell Jim and (I, me) that we're too late!

6. Mrs. Barnes invited the Browns and (we, us) to her party.

7. Mr. Riley, irritated by our loud music, gave Joe and (I, me) a piece of his mind.

8. Tell Ann and (she, her) what you want them to do.

9. The honors list included Jane and (he, him).

10. At least offer (he, him) and (I, me) some consolation.

11. Long hours of hiking tire both Tom and (he, him).

12. Consider the Clarks and (we, us) in your proposal.

13. Will you recommend (he, him) and (I, me) for the jobs?

14. Please play Nancy and (I, me) something on your guitar.

15. We gave Pat and (she, her) some records for Christmas.

16. You'd better consult the Smiths and (they, them) before you go on with the work.

17. Mr. Olson's plan included John and (I, me).

18. Ask John and (she, her) if they can come with us.

19. Don't give Don and (I, me) any more dessert.

20. Please tell Peter and Eric and (he, him) that joke again.

The Pronoun as Object (II)

When the pronoun is the object of a preposition, the objective form is always used. Problems may arise when the object is compound. To decide which pronoun to use, *try each part of the object by itself with the preposition.*

> Mr. Jones offered the jobs to Ann and (I, me).
> (to Ann; to me, *not* to I)

The Pronoun Used with a Noun. In a construction such as *we girls* or *us boys*, the use of the noun determines the case form of the pronoun.

> We girls made our dresses for the party.
> (*girls* is the subject of *made*; the nominative pronoun is therefore required.)

To decide which pronoun form to use in the construction such as *we girls*, try the pronoun by itself with the verb or preposition.

> The hours on the job are too long for (we, us) girls.
> (for us, *not* for we)

Choosing the Correct Pronoun. In each sentence below, underline the correct form of the pronoun.

1. Just between you and (I, me), I'm afraid of flying.
2. Miss Miller doesn't live far from you and (she, her).
3. There has been a good relationship between the Flynns and (we, us) for years.
4. Give the awards to Alice and (he, him).
5. The prize money will be divided among the Clarks, the Smiths, and (we, us).
6. The principal congratulated (we, us) boys!
7. The work was divided among (we, us) men in the club.
8. The master of ceremonies had a special prize for John and (he, him).
9. Please put your trust in Mary and (I, me).
10. The referendum was decided by all of (we, us) voters.
11. I received phone calls from Sarah and (she, her) last night.
12. Everyone was on time for the meeting except (we, us) girls.
13. Please tell your story to Paul and (he, him).
14. The actor sat down beside Joy and (I, me).
15. The reward is meant for the Jensens and (we, us).
16. The basketball center towered above Bob and (she, her).
17. They want to play tennis with (we, us) boys.
18. The clouds drifted lazily above Jane and (I, me).
19. The baseball landed just beyond (we, us) girls.
20. The children played in a circle around Beth and (he, him).

Other Problems with Pronouns

Pronouns in Comparisons. Sometimes a comparison is made by using a clause that begins with *than* or *as*.

> You are better at French *than I am*.
> Jack has as good grades *as she has*.

Sometimes the final clause in the comparison is left incomplete.

> You are better at French than I (am).
> Jack has as good grades as she (has).

To decide which pronoun form to use in an incomplete comparison, complete the comparison.

> Ellen saves more of her paycheck than (I, me).
> (Ellen saves more of her paycheck than I *save*.)

Compound Personal Pronouns. Compound personal pronouns are used only when their antecedents appear in the same sentence.

> NONSTANDARD   The tickets were meant for ourselves.
> STANDARD   The tickets were meant for us.

Choosing the Correct Pronoun. Underline the standard form of the pronoun in each sentence.

> Example: Marge is a better letter writer than (<u>I</u>, me).

1. Terry is a better golfer than (he, him).
2. No restrictions apply to (you, yourself).
3. Betty had a more exciting summer than (I, me).
4. Jim got more financial aid than (I, me).
5. You have a longer assignment than (I, me).
6. Dick hasn't studied as hard as (I, me).
7. Meg is a faster reader than (he, him).
8. We have as long a vacation as (they, them).
9. Does that car belong to (you, yourself)?
10. On his job Frank gets more pay than (I, me).
11. You have a bigger house than (we, us).
12. No one works harder than (she, her).
13. Joe is two years older than (I, me).
14. All the regulations apply to (you, yourself).
15. You have a better chance of winning the award than (I, me).
16. Peg has as much money as (they, them).
17. In our class play Tim was a better actor than (he, him).
18. The award was meant for (me, myself).
19. The Fields play tennis better than (we, us).
20. Nancy is a harder-working class officer than (he, him).

Pronouns and Antecedents

A pronoun agrees with its antecedent in number, gender, and person. If the antecedent is singular, a singular pronoun is required. The plural antecedent requires a plural pronoun. The following antecedents are referred to by singular pronouns: *anybody, anyone, each, either, everybody, everyone, neither, nobody, one, somebody, someone.*

Each of the boys has *his* own savings account.

Singular antecedents joined by *or* or *nor* are referred to by a singular pronoun.

Neither John *nor* Dave could find his ticket.

Collective nouns may take either a singular or plural pronoun, depending on the meaning of the sentence.

The cast is having *its* picture taken.
The cast quickly took *their* places onstage.

Choosing the Right Pronoun. Underline the correct pronoun in each sentence.

Example: Either Frank or Bob will give you (<u>his</u>, their) ticket.

1. Neither Mary nor Laura has turned in (her, their) report.

2. Anybody can learn to set up (his, their) own tent.

3. Each of the boys takes care of (his, their) own room.

4. Neither Tom nor Jim can give (his, their) report today.

5. Anyone can join our group if (he, they) is really interested.

6. The team can't play (its, their) best when it's too hot.

7. Either Bill or Tony will lend you (his, their) book.

8. Everyone should do (his, their) best work on the project.

9. George wants to go into politics; he finds (it, them) exciting.

10. Everyone should be in (his, their) seat before the curtain goes up.

11. Some of the team are wearing (his, their) new helmets.

12. Every class officer will do (her, their) best.

13. I find that playing bridge is hard on (my, your) nerves.

14. Some of the vanilla has lost (its, their) flavor.

15. Everybody will receive (his, their) own copy of the minutes of the meeting.

16. Someone will be disappointed by (his, their) grade on the exam.

17. One should not worry too much about (his, their) past mistakes.

18. Each of us is prepared to give (his, their) speech on Thursday.

19. Has anyone lost (his, their) jacket?

20. Nobody plays (his, their) best when the humidity is very high.

Indefinite Reference

To avoid confusion for the reader, every personal pronoun should refer clearly to a definite antecedent.

INDEFINITE   When the play begins, they don't let you in until the end of the first act.

BETTER   When the play begins, the ushers don't let you in until the end of the first act.

INDEFINITE   They say that *All Creatures Great and Small* is a good book.

BETTER   That book reviewer said that *All Creatures Great and Small* is a good book.

Avoiding Indefinite References. Revise the sentences below to remove all indefinite pronoun references.

Example: It says in the book that Elizabeth I was a great queen.

BETTER: The book says that Elizabeth I was a great queen.

1. You should find out your credit rating if they will let you.

_____

2. In Ireland you're apt to be rained on every day.

_____

3. They try very hard, but it never shows.

_____

4. In the preface it says why the author wrote the book.

_____

5. Helen wants to be an actress because it's such an exciting life.

_____

6. We hailed the taxi driver, but it kept going.

_____

7. In the nineteenth century, you had to work a twelve-hour day.

_____

8. Mrs. Jones writes a good letter, and does it often.

_____

9. In Arizona you get very little rainfall.

_____

10. The luncheon as a whole was good, but they didn't do a very good job with the dessert.

_____

_____

Ambiguous Reference

The reference of a pronoun is ambiguous if the pronoun may refer back to more than one word. *Ambiguous* means "having two or more possible meanings." Ambiguous pronouns confuse the reader because the meaning is not clear.

Bill told Tom his book was lost. (whose book?)

Avoiding Ambiguous References. Revise the sentences below to remove all ambiguous pronoun references.

Example: Add the noodles to the casseroles after cooking them.

BETTER   After cooking the noodles, add them to the casseroles.

1. When Mary spoke with the Premier's wife, she was very polite. _____

2. After we took the dish from the beautifully carved box, it broke. _____

3. We removed the pictures from the walls and washed them. _____

4. Mr. Ling told Jim he would be late for the games. _____

5. Take the tablecloth off the table and wash it. _____

6. Jane told Peg that she had won first prize. _____

7. I put my plant on the shelf, but it still didn't look right. _____

8. Mr. Peterson's article was in the magazine, but I didn't read it. _____

9. On my bicycle I chased the robber's car until it broke down. _____

10. Please take the pan off the stove and wash it. _____

Review: Pronoun Usage   114

Choosing the Correct Pronoun. Underline the correct pronoun in each sentence below.

Example: Millie and (<u>I</u>, me) are going shopping tomorrow.

1. The best athlete in the gym class is (she, her).
2. The stretcher was pushed by the orderly and (he, him).
3. The photographs of the children and (we, us) are blurred.
4. Cindy and (he, him) are riding their bikes to the stadium.
5. Mom served (I, me) a delicious dinner.
6. I need to ask the receptionist or (her, she) where the office is located.
7. That secret was supposed to be kept between you and (I, me).
8. A bill was mistakenly sent to (we, us).
9. Melanie is a faster jogger than (I, me).
10. The packages were to be delivered to (us, ourselves).
11. Either Bud or Larry left (his, their) skateboard at my house.
12. Neither the surgeon nor the doctor has answered (his, their) page.
13. All of the knives need to have (its, their) blades sharpened.
14. None of the neighbors on our block lets (his, their) dog loose.
15. One of the members of the team earned (his, their) letter this week.

Avoiding Ambiguous and Indefinite References. Revise the sentences below to remove all indefinite and ambiguous pronoun references.

Example: They will be putting summer clothes on sale in July.

Sears will be putting summer clothes on sale in July.

1. Be sure to exercise regularly and keep it up. _____

_____

2. We went to a fancy restaurant but it didn't taste that special. _____

_____

3. It was awful on the highway over the weekend. _____

_____

4. The dog and cat were fighting and it got hurt. _____

_____

5. Sally told Ellen that she was wanted in the office immediately. _____

_____

Adverbs with Action Verbs 115

Certain adverbs are formed by adding *-ly* to adjectives: *careful—carefully*. There is sometimes a temptation to use an adjective rather than an adverb.

NONSTANDARD	Dress *warm*.	STANDARD	Dress *warmly*.
	Go *slow*!		Go *slowly*!
	Sing *loud*.		Sing *loudly*.

All of the words used above as adverbs are also used as adjectives: a *quick* trip, a *loud* voice.

Most of the words that may be either adjectives or adverbs are words of one syllable. Adjectives of two or more syllables almost never have the same form for the adverb.

> The *careful* driver has few accidents. (adjective)
> Jane *carefully* measured the coffee. (adverb)

After an action verb, use the *-ly* form of the modifier if the modifier has two or more syllables.

Choosing the Right Modifier. Underline the correct form in each sentence below.

Example: Susan mended her torn jeans (careful, carefully).

1. Mr. Jones called (angry, angrily) to us.
2. The old woman made her way (careful, carefully) up the stairs.
3. Gwen framed the picture (painstaking, painstakingly).
4. I did the assignment (easy, easily).
5. Ms. Owens (quick, quickly) made her way through the crowded hall.
6. Sheila injured her elbow (bad, badly) when she fell.
7. Tim entered the room (cautious, cautiously).
8. Did the man speak (threatening, threateningly) to you?
9. The clerk nodded (cool, coolly) to me when I approached him.
10. Dave is working (steady, steadily) on his project.
11. Sally approached the police officer (calm, calmly).
12. The little boys clattered (noisy, noisily) down the stairs.
13. I can see (clear, clearly) how I should do this problem.
14. Mary will (certain, certainly) be late for the meeting.
15. The two boys talked (quiet, quietly) for an hour.
16. Ann's picture was displayed (prominent, prominently) above the fireplace.
17. Bob stared (moody, moodily) out the window.
18. The lecturer peered (uneasy, uneasily) at the audience.
19. The little girl gazed (shy, shyly) at the Premier's wife.
20. In telling us the news, Sam spoke (sad, sadly).

Adjectives with Linking Verbs   116

Forms of the verb *be* are always used as linking verbs. Other verbs such as *look, sound, appear, feel, smell, stay,* and *grow* may be used as either action verbs followed by adverbs, or as linking verbs. To decide whether a verb is used to link or show action, try substituting a form of *be*. If the sentence still makes sense, the verb is a linking verb and is followed by an adjective.

> EXAMPLE
>
> Cynthia seems rather (*shy,* shyly).
>   (*Cynthia is shyly* does not make sense. *Cynthia is shy* makes sense; *seems* is a linking verb here.)
> Cynthia looked (shy, *shyly*) at the mayor.
>   (*was* does not make sense with either modifier; *looked* is an action verb here.)

Choosing the Right Modifier. Underline the correct form in each sentence below.

1. Tom sounded (angry, angrily) when he spoke to me.
2. Under the heavy blanket I stayed (warm, warmly) all night.
3. The apple pie smells (good, well).
4. The musician sounded his trumpet (loud, loudly).
5. Mrs. Barnes works (good, well) with many people.
6. Bill looks (tired, tiredly) after his ordeal.
7. The peach ice cream tasted (good, well) on that hot night.
8. Have you played the game of smelling several substances (careful, carefully) and then identifying them?
9. The campers stayed (cozy, cozily) by the fire all night.
10. I've learned to identify fabrics blindfolded by feeling them (careful, carefully).
11. The little girl looked (cautious, cautiously) to the right and left.
12. Bob has a hot temper, but he never remains (angry, angrily) very long.
13. Karen tasted the hot chili (cautious, cautiously).
14. The children seem (restless, restlessly) today.
15. Ann seems (anxious, anxiously) about her grade on the test.
16. Don always becomes (angry, angrily) when he's teased about his nickname.
17. After reading by the fire, Ken became very (sleepy, sleepily).
18. The robbery suspect seemed (uneasy, uneasily) when he was questioned.
19. Pam always remains (calm, calmly) under pressure.
20. I looked (uneasy, uneasily) at the judges.

Usage Problems (I)

This, These, Them, That and Those. *This* and *that* modify singular words. *These* and *those* modify plural words. The words *kind, sort,* and *type* require a singular modifier.

Those may be used as either a pronoun or an adjective. *Them* is always a pronoun.

> *This* sort of shoes is too tight for me. (*Not* these sort)
> *Those* are good books. (pronoun)
> *Those* books are good. (adjective)

Using *This, These, Them, That* and *Those*. Underline the correct word.

Example: (<u>That</u>, Those) kind of pizza is my favorite.

1. I like (that, those) sort of television program.
2. (This, These) type of gloves keeps my hands warm.
3. I put (those, them) spoons in the drawer.
4. (That, Those) kind of answer irritates me.
5. Don't you like (this, these) sort of movies?
6. Elizabeth is always angered by (that, those) type of question.
7. Why should you worry about (that, those) kind of remark?
8. Please put (those, them) tools in the garage.
9. Todd prefers (this, these) sort of sandwiches.
10. (That, Those) type of joke is my favorite.

Bad-Badly and Good-Well. *Bad* is always used after linking verbs. (Mr. Smith *felt* bad. The milk *smelled* bad). *Badly* is used after action verbs. (She *sang* badly.)

Good is used only as an adjective to modify nouns and pronouns, never as an adverb. *Well* is an adjective when it means "in good health, of good appearance, or satisfactory." *Well* is used as an adverb when it means that an action was performed properly and expertly.

Using *Bad-Badly* and *Good-Well*. Underline the correct form.

Example: Mike looks (<u>bad</u>, badly).

1. Mrs. Heinz felt (good, well) about her research grant.
2. The potato salad tastes (bad, badly).
3. Mary plays the trumpet (good, well).
4. The news report about the Mideast sounded (bad, badly).
5. Don't feel (bad, badly) about your mistake.
6. In spite of many lessons Jim plays golf (bad, badly).
7. The lawn mower works (good, well) now.
8. The fish smells (bad, badly).
9. I felt (bad, badly) after my long flight.
10. Don't you think the meat tastes (bad, badly)?

Usage Problems (II) 118

Fewer and Less. *Fewer* is used to describe things that can be counted. *Less* refers to quantity or degree.

> There are fewer students taking Latin now.
> This bulb will give less light.

Using *Fewer* and *Less*. Underline the correct word in each sentence below.

1. I have (fewer, less) problems to solve than you do.
2. Mark has (fewer, less) fear of the water than he used to have.
3. These new tools will cause you (fewer, less) worry.
4. Tom had (fewer, less) pages in his report than I did.
5. Beth feels (fewer, less) anxiety now.
6. We have (fewer, less) milk than I thought.
7. Meg has (fewer, less) worries than anyone else I know.
8. There was (fewer, less) rainfall yesterday than we had expected.
9. There are (fewer, less) cases of measles now.
10. (Fewer, Less) people travel by train now.

The Double Negative. A double negative occurs when a negative word is added to a statement that is already negative. The double negative is nonstandard usage.

> NONSTANDARD   Tom didn't have no book.
>   STANDARD   Tom didn't have any book.

Hardly, used with a negative word, is nonstandard.

> NONSTANDARD   There wasn't hardly any money in my checking account.
>   STANDARD   There was hardly any money in my checking account.

Avoiding the Double Negative. In the following sentences, underline the correct form.

1. We don't have (any, no) groceries.
2. There (was, wasn't) hardly enough ice cream left for lunch.
3. I don't have (any, no) money.
4. He doesn't know (anything, nothing) about sailing.
5. I (could, couldn't) hardly see the stage.
6. There (was, wasn't) hardly anything I could do to help.
7. Larry doesn't have (a, no) car.
8. We (had, hadn't) hardly enough heat last winter.
9. Helen doesn't care (anything, nothing) about golf.
10. I don't see (anything, nothing) moving in the bushes.

Comparisons

Comparative and Superlative. The comparative form of a modifier is used to compare only two things; the superlative is used to compare three or more things. The comparative is made either by adding an *-er* ending or by using the word *more*. The superlative is formed either by adding *-est* or by using the word *most*. Never use *more* or *most* if you have already added the *-er* or *-est* ending.

Using Comparisons. Circle the mistakes in the following sentences. Place the correct form in the blank.

1. Do you like *Canadian Living* or *Gourmet* best? _____
2. For your report you can read either *Tom Sawyer* or *Huckleberry Finn*, but I think you'll like *Tom Sawyer* best. _____
3. Jim is more taller than Don. _____
4. Ms. Gordon is the most busiest of the three bank officers. _____
5. Of the two schools, Central has the biggest enrollment. _____
6. Alice is the more calmer of the two girls. _____
7. Which of the two programs do you like best? _____
8. Mike is the heavier player on the football team. _____
9. What would be the more interesting job in the world? _____
10. Mary is the most dependable of the two girls. _____

Illogical Comparisons. When an individual is compared with the rest of the group, always use the word *other* or the word *else*.

> Jim is more vocal than any of the officers.
> (Is Jim an officer, too?)
> Jim is more vocal than any of the *other* officers. (*other* tells you he is.)

State both parts of a comparison completely if the meaning is not clear.

> I listen to the radio more than my sister.
> (I listen to my sister? My sister listens to the radio?)
> I listen to the radio more than my sister listens to it. (logical)

Avoiding Illogical Comparisons. Add a word or words needed to make the following sentences logical rather than illogical comparisons.

1. Rex is more punctual than any of the students. _____
2. Beth watches television more than Ann. _____
3. Dave has more patience than any boy I know. _____
4. Our team has won more games than any team in the league. _____
5. Mike is more talkative than any boy in the club. _____
6. Ms. Persons gives harder tests than any teacher in the school. _____
7. Mr. Bucks is richer than anyone in our town. _____
8. Al has more hobbies than anyone I know. _____
9. Physics is more difficult than any subject offered in school. _____
10. Football games attract more spectators than any sport. _____

Review: Adjective and Adverb Usage   120

Choosing the Right Modifier. Underline the correct form in each sentence below.

Example: We walked (brisk, <u>briskly</u>) through the forest.

1. I need to wash my hair (desperate, desperately).
2. You must do the computations (careful, carefully).
3. The cab driver seemed (uncertain, uncertainly) about our destination.
4. The harvest appears (meager, meagerly) this year.
5. We looked (eager, eagerly) at the surprise package.
6. Lynne looked (tired, tiredly) after her day on the job.
7. (This, These) sort of cookies is my favorite.
8. John felt (well, good) about scoring the winning run.
9. Surprisingly, the sandwiches looked (good, well) before we ate them.
10. The accident sounded (bad, badly) as it was reported on the radio.
11. Do you prefer (that, those) type of tires to radials?
12. The Canadiens played (good, well) the night we saw them.
13. The picture appeared (crooked, crookedly) from where we stood.
14. Nancy's test paper is (perfect, perfectly).
15. All the girls looked (jealous, jealously) when Tom asked Sally to the dance.

Choosing the Right Modifier. Underline the correct form in each sentence below.

Example: I eat (fewer, <u>less</u>) candy since the dentist filled my teeth.

1. Don't you have (any, no) live bait for fishing?
2. (Fewer, Less) cars were on the road than usual.
3. No one (was, wasn't) waiting at the bus stop when I got there.
4. I don't think (anyone, no one) signed up for the clean-up committee.
5. Which burns up (fewer, less) calories—jogging or jumping rope?

Using Comparisons. Find the mistakes in the following sentences. If an extra word has been used, cross it out. If a comparative or superlative has been used incorrectly, circle it and place the correct form in the blank.

Example: Ken is the ⃝most intelligent of the two boys. _more_

1. Of all the cafeteria workers, Mrs. Brown is the nicer. _____
2. Which do you like better—apple, cherry, or blueberry pie? _____
3. What is the most tallest building in your downtown area? _____
4. Considering all of the contestants, I deserved to win more. _____
5. Getting a blood test hurts lesser than getting a shot. _____

The Past Forms of Verbs (I)

Most of the several thousand English verbs cause no problems of usage at all. They are **regular verbs.** That is, the past tense is formed by adding *-ed* or *-d* to the present, and the past participle is the same as the past tense form:

PRESENT	PAST	PAST PARTICIPLE
walk	walked	walked
dance	danced	danced

There are about sixty commonly used verbs, however, whose past forms do not follow this pattern. They are **irregular verbs.**

One group of irregular verbs has the same form for the past and the past participle:

PRESENT	PAST	PAST PARTICIPLE	PRESENT	PAST	PAST PARTICIPLE
bring	brought	brought	lend	lent	lent
catch	caught	caught	lose	lost	lost
dive	dived or dove	dived	say	said	said
fight	fought	fought	shine	shone	shone
flee	fled	fled	sit	sat	sat
fling	flung	flung	sting	stung	stung
get	got	got or gotten	swing	swung	swung
lead	led	led			

The past tense form is always used alone. The past participle form is used with forms of *be* or *have*.

I *gave* the man some money.   I *have given* the man some money.

Using Verbs Correctly. In the sentences below, the present form of a verb is given in parentheses. Substitute either past or past participle, whichever the sentence requires.

Example: The major has (fight) in three wars. ___*fought*___

1. The officer (lead) his troops to safety yesterday. _____

2. I (lend) Ken a book three weeks ago. _____

3. I hope that you have (bring) me some good news. _____

4. We have finally (sit) down after standing in line for an hour. _____

5. Have you (catch) many fish? _____

6. The hostages (flee) from their captors last night. _____

7. Have you (get) any stamps at the post office yet? _____

8. The baseball player (swing) wildly at the ball. _____

9. I hope you weren't (sting) by that bee! _____

10. I'm afraid Ken has (lose) that book he borrowed from me. _____

The Past Forms of Verbs (II)

Another group of irregular verbs adds *n* or *en* to the past form to make the past participle:

PRESENT	PAST	PAST PARTICIPLE	PRESENT	PAST	PAST PARTICIPLE
bear	bore	borne	speak	spoke	spoken
beat	beat	beaten	steal	stole	stolen
bite	bit	bitten	swear	swore	sworn
break	broke	broken	tear	tore	torn
choose	chose	chosen	wear	wore	worn
freeze	froze	frozen			

Using Verbs Correctly. In the following sentences, the present form of the verb is given in parentheses. Substitute either past or past participle, whichever the sentence requires.

Example: The water in the pond has (freeze). ___*frozen*___

1. Sue (wear) her best dress last night for the party. _____

2. Tim lost a filling when he (bite) into the hard peanut brittle. _____

3. The judge has (swear) to uphold the constitution. _____

4. The old man has (bear) his many troubles bravely. _____

5. Your football team has (beat) ours for three years in a row. _____

6. In her speech at assembly Marge (speak) clearly and calmly. _____

7. Which prize have you (choose)? _____

8. Our principal has never (break) a promise to us. _____

9. Dave (tear) up the note he received yesterday. _____

10. A pickpocket has (steal) my wallet. _____

11. We haven't (break) any cups since we bought our new set of china.

_____

12. The ice cubes have (freeze) already. _____

13. Sally hasn't (speak) to me since last week. _____

14. Michael's family (bear) the expense of his college education. _____

15. Mrs. O'Neill (wear) her fur coat many times last winter. _____

16. I'm afraid that someone (steal) my notebook. _____

17. Ms. Mitchell (choose) the first two weeks in August for her vacation.

_____

18. Pete (bite) into the candy bar greedily. _____

19. Your baseball team (beat) mine yesterday. _____

20. Vito has (tear) his new shirt. _____

The Past Forms of Verbs (III)

Seven irregular verbs are alike and follow the same pattern in changing the middle vowel: *swim, swam, swum,* for example. Here are the verbs that follow this pattern:

PRESENT	PAST	PAST PARTICIPLE
begin	began	begun
drink	drank	drunk
ring	rang	rung
sing	sang	sung
sink	sank or sunk	sunk
spring	sprang or sprung	sprung
swim	swam	swum

Using Verbs Correctly. In the following sentences, the present form of the verb is given in parentheses. Substitute the past or past participle, whichever makes the sentence correct. Remember, the past participle always has a helping verb.

Example: Have you (ring) the doorbell? _____ *rung* _____

1. Nancy (swim) well in yesterday's race. _____
2. Ann hasn't (begin) to think about her choice of college yet. _____
3. I think Dave (sing) well in tryouts last week. _____
4. We must have (drink) a gallon of iced tea that hot day! _____
5. Mr. Jensen (begin) refinishing his coffee table last night. _____
6. I had (ring) the doorbell just once when Mr Johnston came to the door. _____
7. Many ships have (sink) off the coast of Newfoundland. _____
8. I have never (swim) in the ocean before. _____
9. From the shore we watched as the abandoned sailboat slowly (sink).

_____

10. I was frightened when the dog (spring) at me. _____
11. Tim has (sing) in every musical our school has given. _____
12. Barbara has always (drink) a glass of milk with every meal. _____
13. I know that I should have (begin) work on my project before this.

_____

14. René has (swim) in every swimming meet this year. _____
15. The water between the mainland and the island is called "Death's Door" because so many ships have (sink) there. _____
16. Al's rowboat has (spring) a leak. _____
17. The church bells (ring) all morning when the end of the fighting was announced. _____
18. When he was younger, Sam (sing) tenor, but now he sings bass. _____
19. I would have (drink) the tea if it hadn't been too hot. _____
20. Have you (begin) painting your room yet? _____

The Past Forms of Verbs (IV)

Another group of irregular verbs makes the past participle from the present form, not the past form:

PRESENT	PAST	PAST PARTICIPLE	PRESENT	PAST	PAST PARTICIPLE
blow	blew	blown	know	knew	known
come	came	come	ride	rode	ridden
do	did	done	rise	rose	risen
draw	drew	drawn	run	ran	run
drive	drove	driven	see	saw	seen
eat	ate	eaten	shake	shook	shaken
fall	fell	fallen	slay	slew	slain
give	gave	given	take	took	taken
go	went	gone	throw	threw	thrown
grow	grew	grown	write	wrote	written

Using Verbs Correctly. In the following sentences, underline the correct form of the verb.

Example: I have never (drove, <u>driven</u>) to Sault St. Marie.

1. Sarah has (blew, blown) out all the candles on her birthday cake.

2. I have never (drew, drawn) an absolutely straight line in my life.

3. I'm afraid your car has (ran, run) out of gas.

4. Ryan (rided, rode) horseback in the parade.

5. Have you (took, taken) out the garbage?

6. Meg has (grew, grown) up to be a brilliant attorney.

7. The bandit was (slew, slayed, slain) as he tried to escape.

8. I hope you (came, come) to pick up your book yesterday.

9. What have I (did, done) to deserve that punishment?

10. Has Bob really (ate, eaten) all that ice cream?

11. At dawn they (saw, seen) the top of the mountain.

12. The Browns have (went, gone) to Vancouver for their vacation.

13. I don't think that John Steinbeck has ever (wrote, written) a better book than *The Pearl*.

14. Has Carrie ever (drove, driven) to Florida?

15. I have never (knew, known) a more patient person than Ann.

16. Bill was (threw, thrown) from his horse during the parade.

17. Mr. Rogers has never (gave, given) much to charity.

18. The sun (rised, rose) at 5:30 yesterday morning.

19. Bill had never (fell, fallen) while riding before.

20. Have you ever (shook, shaken) hands with the mayor?

The Past Forms of Verbs (V) 125

In the following sentences, the present form of the verb is given in parentheses. Substitute the past or past participle, whichever makes the sentence correct. Remember, the past participle always has a helping verb.

Example: I (throw) out all my old letters yesterday. _*threw*_

1. The principal (come) to the point of her speech very quickly. _____

2. Tim has (be) in every track meet this year. _____

3. Mahatma Gandhi (know) what it meant to be hungry. _____

4. The watchman was (slay) while he was making his rounds. _____

5. How long has it (take) you to paint the kitchen? _____

6. How many people (run) for Mayor in the last election? _____

7. All the plants at the flower show were (grow) by members of the Garden Club. _____

8. It doesn't seem possible that we could have (eat) so fast! _____

9. The noon whistle has (blow) every day since 1937. _____

10. What have you (do) with your ticket? _____

11. The wind (blow) down lots of branches last night. _____

12. Robert has never (give) up in his try for the boxing title. _____

13. We had (drive) through the night to reach Saskatoon. _____

14. Dan got up as soon as the sun (rise) today. _____

15. How would you have (draw) the boundary lines between the provinces? _____

16. Martha was badly (shake) by her experience. _____

17. Nancy's hands (shake) as she reached for her diploma. _____

18. Ms. Ellison never (drive) her car faster than eighty kilometres an hour. _____

19. How far have you (ride) on your bicycle? _____

20. Janet has never (see) an opera. _____

21. I have (write) Jane twice in the last week. _____

22. Stan has (take) fifty pictures on his vacation. _____

23. Did you know that Elaine (go) home early yesterday? _____

24. Cora has (see) the movie *Jaws* three times. _____

25. Our committee chairman has (do) his best; now it's up to us. _____

Using *Lie* and *Lay*

The verb *lay* means "to put or place something." The verb lie has eight or nine meanings, all having in common the idea of "being in a horizontal position, or to remain, or to be situated."

Lie is always an intransitive verb. That is, it never has an object. *Lay* is a transitive verb. It almost always has an object. The principal parts of these verbs are as follows:

PRESENT	PAST	PAST PARTICIPLE
lay	laid	laid
lie	lay	lain

Using *Lie* and *Lay* Correctly. In the following sentences, underline the correct form of *lay* or *lie*.

Example: Mrs. Norman (<u>lay</u>, laid) down for a nap an hour ago.

1. Please (lie, lay) the cloth on the table.

2. Ms. Stouffer told us to (lie, lay) our work aside.

3. Will you (lie, lay) down for a rest this afternoon?

4. I think we've (lain, laid) our plans well.

5. (Lie, Lay) your books beside mine.

6. The doctor (lay, laid) all my fears to rest when she talked to me yesterday.

7. The button from my jacket was (lying, laying) on the sidewalk.

8. I'm afraid that Tim has been (lying, laying) down on the job.

9. Every evening Sue (lies, lays) her clothes out for the next day.

10. The chickens (lay, laid) more eggs than usual yesterday.

11. Can you help me (lie, lay) the floor in the bathroom?

12. I have (lain, laid) the key somewhere, and now I can't find it.

13. When Mr. Jones (lay, laid) down for a nap, he was unable to sleep.

14. My pen was (lying, laying) on the table.

15. Mr. Brown (lay, laid) his briefcase on the table when he entered.

16. Miss Jenkins is so tired that she's been (lying, laying) down all afternoon.

17. I (lay, laid) the book aside and answered the doorbell.

18. Our dog never (lies, lays) down when told to do so.

19. The blame for the mistake has been (lain, laid) on my shoulders.

20. Your jacket has been (lying, laying) on the floor all morning.

Using *Sit* and *Set*

The verb *sit* means "to rest with the legs bent and the back upright," but there are many other related meanings. The verb *set* means "to put or place something."

Sit is an intransitive verb; it never has an object. *Set* is a transitive verb; it almost always has an object. The principal parts are as follows:

PRESENT	PAST	PAST PARTICIPLE
sit	sat	sat
set	set	set

Using *Sit* and *Set* Correctly. In the following sentences, underline the correct form of *sit* or *set*.

Example: (Sit, <u>Set</u>) the plate on the table.

1. (Sit, Set) down and rest while you have a chance.

2. The boat (sat, set) sail into the West.

3. After being away from home so long, I had forgotten how to (sit, set) the table.

4. I find it relaxing to (sit, set) in a rocking chair.

5. (Sit, Set) aside some time for studying.

6. After (sitting, setting) down to watch TV, Joe fell asleep.

7. After (sitting, setting) up all night on the bus, Mrs. Clark is exhausted.

8. I know you'll do good work if you (sit, set) your mind to it.

9. She asked me to (sit, set) down and talk with her.

10. Don't you ever get tired of just (sitting, setting) around?

11. Have you (sat, set) the date for the picnic?

12. Mr. Gillis hasn't had time to (sit, set) down all day.

13. I hope that my decision will (sit, set) your mind at rest.

14. (Sitting, Setting) by the campfire, Bob soon became too warm.

15. The former Prime Minister now (sits, sets) in the House of Lords.

16. Have you ever (sat, set) to have your portrait painted?

17. My sister (set, sat) the school record for cross-country running.

18. Amos is tired of (sitting, setting) on the sidelines.

19. The jeweler (sat, set) the price of the diamond at five hundred dollars.

20. John had (sat, set) his heart on winning the race.

Using *Rise* and *Raise*

The verb *rise* means "to go to a higher position." The verb *raise* means "to lift to a higher position."

Rise is intransitive; it never has an object. *Raise* is transitive; it almost always has an object. Things *rise* by themselves; they are *raised* by something else. The principal parts of these verbs are as follows:

PRESENT	PAST	PAST PARTICIPLE
rise	rose	risen
raise	raised	raised

Using *Rise* and *Raise* Correctly. In the following sentences, underline the correct form of *rise* or *raise* given in parentheses.

Example: Our neighbors (rise, <u>raise</u>) their flag every morning.

1. Will our taxes (rise, raise) again this year?

2. Ms. Arity (rose, raised) her voice above the commotion in the room.

3. The price of coffee continues to (rise, raise).

4. Has the bread (risen, raised)?

5. The river (rises, raises) each spring.

6. The principal (rose, raised) no objection to our plan.

7. Our rent has (risen, raised) again this year.

8. Do you think the landlord will (rise, raise) our rent this year?

9. The banner was (risen, raised) above our heads.

10. Tom is so depressed that it will be hard to (rise, raise) his spirits.

11. The Fergusons (rise, raise) dairy cattle on their farm.

12. Do you think the grocery stores will (rise, raise) the price of milk?

13. We all (rose, raised) from our seats when the band played the national anthem.

14. It was Mr. Bruce's ambition to (rise, raise) higher in the company.

15. Carol (rose, raised) at six o'clock this morning.

16. The colonial army (rose, raised) in revolt against the British.

17. Much protest has (risen, raised) against the higher prices of cars.

18. The sun (rose, raised) at six this morning.

19. Mr. Corso (rose, raised) the flag in front of the school.

20. Mr. Morton always said that he had (rose, raised) his children to be law-abiding citizens.

Review: Verb Usage

Using Verbs Correctly. In the sentences below, the present form of a verb is given in parentheses. Substitute either past or past participle, whichever the sentence requires.

Example: The captain (lead) his troops into battle. _*led*_

1. Who (bring) those delicious cookies? _____

2. The shortstop (catch) the ball on the edge of the infield grass. _____

3. Lisa (dive) gracefully into the pool. _____

4. The vagabond (fling) his knapsack over his shoulder. _____

5. Have you (get) your diploma yet? _____

6. Mitch (lend) me his gym shorts for the game. _____

7. The scorching sun (shine) for days without relief. _____

8. I was (sting) by two bees during the picnic. _____

9. Minorities have (bear) the burden of prejudice for decades. _____

10. Our team was badly (beat) in the semifinals. _____

11. I thought for a long time before I (choose) my prize. _____

12. Last year the lake was (freeze) all the way across. _____

13. They told me not to speak until (speak) to. _____

14. We were all (swear) to secrecy about the surprise party. _____

15. I have (tear) my sweater at the elbow. _____

16. After the music had (begin), I felt in a better mood. _____

17. I was awake, but the alarm clock had not yet (ring). _____

18. The window shade (spring) up, frightening everyone. _____

19. The strong wind has (shake) all the leaves off the trees. _____

20. The youngster has (grow) five centimetres during the year. _____

Using *Lie* and *Lay*, *Sit* and *Set*, and *Raise* and *Rise* Correctly. In each sentence, underline the correct form.

Example: I (lay, laid) in bed for hours before I fell asleep.

1. The custodian will (rise, raise) the flag before school opens.

2. There were toys (lying, laying) all over the floor.

3. (Sit, Set) down and talk to me for a while, please.

4. The pizza dough has (raised, risen).

5. The florist (lay, laid) the flowers in the box.

Using Standard English (I)

Many pages in this book are concerned with problems of usage. They present choices of words and constructions that are accepted as **standard usage**—the kind of usage that is appropriate at all times and in all places.

Some forms and constructions are marked **nonstandard usage.** While these may go unchallenged or unnoticed in the locker room, they are nonstandard because they are not acceptable everywhere. In many situations they mark the user as careless or untrained in the English language.

agree to, agree with, agree on You agree *to* something such as a plan of action. You agree *with* someone else. Or, something such as spinach does not agree *with* you. You agree with others *on* a course of action.

anywhere, nowhere, somewhere These are the standard forms. *Anywheres, nowheres, somewheres* are nonstandard.

all right The misspelling *alright* is nonstandard usage. The two words are separate.

altogether, all together *Altogether* means entirely or on the whole. *All together* means that all parts of a group are considered at once.

> Your theory is *altogether* mistaken. (entirely)
> *All together* we marched into the mayor's office.

Using Standard English. Choose the standard form from the two choices given for each sentence below. Underline the standard form.

Example: Helen put her book down (<u>somewhere,</u> somewheres), and now she can't find it.

1. Cucumbers have never (agreed to, agreed with, agreed on) me.
2. (All right, Alright), I'll go with you.
3. Susan can't find her bracelet (anywhere, anywheres).
4. The account of our meeting was (altogether, all together) wrong.
5. Betty could find her lost book (nowhere, nowheres).
6. Tom is feeling (all right, alright) again after the flu.
7. We found the old coins (altogether, all together) in the desk drawer.
8. Did you put your new record (somewhere, somewheres)?
9. That is (altogether, all together) another story; I'll tell it to you later.
10. The members of the committee (agreed to, agreed with, agreed on) what should be done.
11. (All right, Alright), I'll get back to work now.
12. I'm afraid I can't (agree to, agree with, agree on) your proposal.
13. After discussing our choice of restaurants, Sue said, "I'll go (anywhere, anywheres) you like."
14. (Altogether, All together) there were ten of us at the party.
15. (All right, Alright), I'll go to the movie with you.

Using Standard English (II)

among, between *Between* expresses the joining or separation of two people or things. *Among* refers to a group of three or more.

NONSTANDARD   Let's divide this casserole *among* the two of us.
STANDARD   **Let's divide this casserole *between* the two of us.**

amount, number *Amount* is used to indicate a total sum of things. It is usually used to refer to items that cannot be counted. *Number* is used to refer to items that can be counted.

The *amount* of lemonade we drank at the picnic is hard to believe.
The *number* of glasses of lemonade we drank at the picnic is hard to believe.

angry at, angry with You are angry *with* a person and angry *at* a thing.

beside, besides *Beside* means at the side of. *Besides* means in addition to.

Bob sat *beside* Linda at the play.
I can think of other risks *besides* that one.

differ from, differ with One thing or person differs *from* another in characteristics. You differ *with* someone when you disagree with him or her.

in, into *In* means inside something. *Into* tells of motion from the outside to the inside of something.

NONSTANDARD   Tom ran *in* the post office.
STANDARD   Tom ran *into* the post office.

kind of a, sort of a   the *a* is unnecessary.

NONSTANDARD   What sort of a coat did you buy?
STANDARD   What sort of coat did you buy?

Using Standard English. Underline the standard form.

1. The three boys divided the cookies (among, between) themselves.
2. Who is coming to the meeting (beside, besides) you?
3. Jean hurried (in, into) the bank ten minutes before it closed.
4. Tony (differs from, differs with) Jack in hair color.
5. The Martins have bought an expensive (kind of a, kind of) car.
6. The (amount, number) of people at the play was amazing.
7. I was (angry at, angry with) the superintendent's announcement.
8. Mike walked (beside, besides) Janet in the graduation ceremonies.
9. What (sort of a, sort of) book do you like best?
10. Paul and Joe divided the French coins (among, between) themselves.
11. The (amount, number) of money Pat spends on records is surprising.
12. I'm really not (angry at, angry with) you.
13. I (differ from, differ with) you about the zoning policy.
14. The little boy ran (in, into) the garage to pick up the rake.
15. What (kind of a, kind of) sundae did you order?

Words Often Misused (I)

accept, except   To *accept* is to agree to something or to receive something willingly. To *except* is to exclude or omit. As a preposition, *except* means "but" or "excluding."

> John *accepted* his new job in May.
> If you do the required work, we will *except* you from this ruling. (verb)
> Every girl *except* Kate wore low heels. (preposition)

borrow, lend.   You borrow *from* someone. You lend *to* someone.

> NONSTANDARD   Please *borrow* me a dictionary.
> STANDARD   Please *lend* me your dictionary.
> STANDARD   May I borrow your dictionary?

bring, take   *Bring* means motion toward someone or some place; *take* means motion away from someone or some place.

> Our mail carrier will not *bring* us mail on Labour Day.
> Peg will *take* the dog home.

can, may   *Can* means able to do something. *May* is used to ask or to grant permission. It also expresses the probability of something happening.

> *May* I go to the movie? (permission)
> *Can* you understand French? (ability)
> It *may* rain this afternoon. (probability)

Could is the past tense of *can*; *might* is the past tense of *may*.

formally, formerly   *Formally* means in a formal manner. *Formerly* means previously.

> Ms. Conroy was *formerly* a gym teacher. She dressed *formally* for the party.

Using the Right Word. Underline the right word.

1. Everyone (accept, except) Jim was seasick when crossing the channel.
2. Will you (borrow, lend) us your rake?
3. (Can, May) you play chess?
4. Even in the jungles some of the British officers dressed (formally, formerly) for dinner.
5. Sue (accepted, excepted) the reward gratefully.
6. After the party I (brought, took) the borrowed dishes back to Robert.
7. I (accept, except) your kind invitation.
8. You've worked so hard this morning that you (can, may) take the afternoon off.
9. Our lawyer was (formally, formerly) a teacher.
10. Our newsboy will (bring, take) us the paper this morning.
11. Please (borrow, lend) me your typewriter.
12. Mr. Jones fully (accepts, excepts) the blame.
13. (Can, May) you do this crossword puzzle?

hanged, hung   Criminals are *hanged*. Things are *hung* on the wall, hooks, or elsewhere.

> He was *hanged* for his part in the rebellion.
> I *hung* my jacket on a hook by the back door.

imply, infer   A speaker or writer suggests or *implies* something. The reader, listener, or observer comes to a conclusion or *infers* something on the basis of what he sees and hears.

> The candidate *implied* that his opponent had been dishonest.
> I *infer* that you oppose the Premier's policy.

leave, let   *Leave* means to go away from. *Let* means permit. The principal parts are *leave, left, left,* and *let, let, let.*

> NONSTANDARD   Please *leave* the dog come in.
> STANDARD   Please *let* the dog come in.
> NONSTANDARD   We should have *left* Ellen come to the meeting.
> STANDARD   We should have *let* Ellen come to the meeting.

majority   This word can be used only with items that can be counted. It is incorrectly used in speaking of time or distance.

> NONSTANDARD   The *majority* of his vacation was spent in playing golf.
> STANDARD   *Most* of his vacation was spent in playing golf.

Using the Right Word. Choose the right word for each sentence below. Underline the word.

> Example: Three pictures were (hanged, <u>hung</u>) by the fireplace.

1. (The majority, Most) of January was extremely cold.
2. (Leave, Let) me know what you decide.
3. My boss (implied, inferred) that I would get a raise.
4. I (imply, infer) from what you say that you are against the proposal.
5. (Leave, Let) the golf ball lie where it is.
6. (The majority, Most) of the dinner was very good.
7. Will you (leave, let) me go camping?
8. Mr. Tilden (implied, inferred) that he doubted my reason for being late.
9. The basket was (hanged, hung) on the porch.
10. I'll (leave, let) you know what my plans are.
11. I (imply, infer) from Blackstone's book that he favors more aid to Turkey.
12. The murderer was (hanged, hung) at daybreak.
13. We have (hanged, hung) the flag out.
14. Please (leave, let) us have our class outside today.
15. (The majority, Most) of the road to Montreal is a four-lane highway.

Review: The Right Word

Using Standard English. Choose the standard form from the two choices given for each sentence below. Underline the standard form.

Example: The family was (altogether, <u>all together</u>) for Christmas.

1. Our club members can't (agree with, agree on) a motto.

2. We didn't have (anywhere, anywheres) special to spend the evening.

3. The boss told her staff that it was (alright, all right) to leave early.

4. Your hypothesis is (all together, altogether) possible.

5. The gym teacher came (among, between) the two fighting boys.

6. There was a large (amount, number) of ants near the picnic blanket.

7. The students were (angry at, angry with) the new school dress code.

8. The football captain sits (beside, besides) the homecoming queen.

9. Sounds in French (differ with, differ from) those in English.

10. We sprinted (in, into) the locker room for our showers.

11. What (kind of a, kind of) sandwich do you have today?

12. Dad is (excepting, accepting) a new job with his firm.

13. No one (except, accept) the immediate family is allowed.

14. No one was willing to (lend, borrow) me money for bus fare.

15. Whom is Bobby (bringing, taking) to the junior prom?

16. I wonder if we (can, may) borrow the Smiths' boat for the weekend.

17. The coach was (formally, formerly) a teacher at Central High.

18. The wet bathing suits were (hanged, hung) over the balcony railing.

19. The master of ceremonies (implied, inferred) that he was nervous too.

20. My parents won't (let, leave) me go camping with my friends.

21. The family spent (most, the majority) of the weekend on the ski slopes.

22. The mewing kitten was (left, let) inside when it began to rain.

23. I dropped all of my books while going (in, into) class.

24. A fight began (among, between) all of the players.

25. I have answered all of the questions (except, accept) one.

A.D., B.C., I, and First Words

A.D., B.C., I. Capitalize the abbreviations *A.D.* and *B.C.*, and the pronoun *I*. The abbreviations *B.C.* and *A.D.* occur only with the number of a year; 457 *B.C.*, *A.D.* 1215.

First Words. Capitalize the first word of a sentence, a direct quotation, and a line of poetry.

> "How do you know you won't run when the time comes?" asked the youth.
> "Run?" said the loud one; "run—of course not." He laughed.
> From *The Red Badge of Courage* by Stephen Crane

> He clasps the crag with crooked hands;
> Close to the sun in lonely lands,
> Ringed with the azure world, he stands.
> From "The Eagle" by Alfred, Lord Tennyson

Capitalizing Words Correctly. Supply capital letters where needed in the items below.

Example: Columbus discovered America in a.d. 1492. *(a.d. corrected to A.D.)*

1. "i'm sorry," said Amy, "that i'm late for your party."
2. success is counted sweetest
   by those who ne'er succeed
   to comprehend a nectar
   requires sorest need.
   Emily Dickinson
3. Rome was settled in 753 b. c.
4. Todd asked, "who won the game yesterday?"
5. all that i know
       of a certain star
   is, it can throw
       (like the angled spar)
   now a dart of red
       now a dart of blue
   From "My Star" by Robert Browning
6. Alexander the Great, the first world conqueror, was born in 356 b. c.
7. "who is to blame for this mistake?" asked Mr. Smith.
8. Debby said softly, "i'll see who is at the door."
9. hark to the whimper of the sea-gull;
   he weeps because he's not an ea-gull.
   suppose you were, you silly sea-gull,
   could you explain it to your she-gull?
   From "The Sea-Gull," by Ogden Nash

Proper Nouns and Adjectives (I)   136

What Are Proper Nouns and Proper Adjectives; A **Common noun** is the name of a whole group of persons, places, or things. A **proper noun** is the name of an individual person, place, or thing. A **proper adjective** is an adjective formed from a proper noun.

COMMON NOUN	PROPER NOUN	PROPER ADJECTIVE
country	France	French
province	Nova Scotia	Nova Scotian

Geographical Names. In a geographical name, capitalize the first letter of each word except articles and prepositions.

The article *the* appearing before a geographical name is not part of the geographical name and is therefore not capitalized.

CONTINENTS   Europe, North America, Africa
BODIES OF WATER   the Pacific Ocean, Lake Michigan, the Red River
LAND FORMS   Mount Everest, the Rocky Mountains, the Laurentians
POLITICAL UNITS   North West Territories, Town of Caledon, Province of Québec, the Department of Agriculture
PUBLIC AREAS   Algonquin Provincial Park, Fort York, Quetico Superior National Park
ROADS AND HIGHWAYS   The Lion's Gate Bridge, Highway 400

Capitalizing Words Correctly. Supply capital letters where needed in the following sentences.

1. Our family has vacationed near lake superior for many years.

2. Shakespeare was born in stratford-on-avon, england.

3. edinburgh, scotland, is located near a body of water called the firth of forth.

4. One of the main highways in ontario is the queen elizabeth.

5. A french airliner crashed in the sahara desert in 1960.

6. The highest mountain peak in the world is mount everest in the himalayan range.

7. Who is the present provincial minister of the department of health and welfare?

8. Which is the longer river—the nile in africa or the mississippi in the united states?

9. We drove on the trans canada all the way from ottawa to vancouver.

10. Mrs. Watkins plans to vacation in the west indies next year.

11. Did you know that vancouver is the capital of british columbia?

12. Tom has seen most of the french battlefields, but he has never visited holland.

Proper Nouns and Adjectives (II) 137

Common Nouns in Names. A common noun that is part of a name is capitalized. A common noun used to define or refer to a proper noun is not capitalized.

PART OF THE NAME	REFERENCE OR DEFINITION
Québec Province	the province of Québec
Québec City	the city of Québec
the Berlin Wall	a wall in Berlin
the Ottawa Valley	the valley of the Ottawa

Words Modified by Proper Adjectives. The word modified by a proper adjective is not capitalized unless adjective and noun together are a geographical name.

GEOGRAPHICAL NAME	MODIFIED NOUN
Arabian Sea	Arabian customs
the Irish Sea	Irish linen
East Germany	Italian dressing

Capitalizing Words Correctly. Supply capital letters where needed in these sentences.

Example: We visited niagara falls in ontario.

1. The gaelic language is still spoken in parts of ireland.
2. We plan to sail down the st. lawrence river
3. Have you ever been to the sequoia national park in california?
4. Many people have attempted to swim the english channel.
5. Barbara's aunt has lived in regina for fifteen years.
6. A famous tourist attraction in british columbia is butchart gardens.
7. The actors tried to use an english accent in the play.
8. My mother brought me some belgian lace from her trip to europe.
9. Madge has never visited the province of manitoba.
10. The debaters have gone to a tournament in three hills, alberta.
11. Two of the countries behind the iron curtain are poland and hungary.
12. Digging the canal through panama took many years.
13. We had our choice of french or italian dressing for our salads.
14. I was seasick when we crossed the english channel.
15. Peg has been in the province of québec, but she has never been in québec city.
16. Cartier, a french navigator, discovered the st. lawrence river.
17. Dan has studied both latin and french.
18. The golden gate bridge in san francisco was completed in 1937.
19. Did you know that greenland is the largest island in the world?
20. lake superior is about 592.8 km long.

Directions and Sections

Always capitalize names of sections of the country, and proper adjectives derived from them. Never capitalize directions of the compass, or adjectives derived from them.

the Maritimes	a north wind
the Southern states	an eastbound flight
Southern cooking	a wind from the north
West Coast	heading to the west

Capitalizing Words Correctly. Remembering what you have learned so far, supply capital letters where needed in the following sentences.

Example: There has been a severe drought in the *W*est this year.

1. The northeast had its coldest winter in one hundred years this year.

2. Keith's grandfather moved west to manitoba in 1920.

3. From paris, Mrs. Elliott will travel south to madrid.

4. The members from the western provinces are especially interested in the welfare of the oil industry.

5. My sister graduated from an eastern college in 1979.

6. The laurentian mountains lie in the southeastern part of the country.

7. The Barnes family has lived in the east for many years.

8. Mrs. Mancuso's firm does more business in the north than in the south.

9. By six o'clock tonight I'll be on a southbound flight.

10. *Sunset Magazine* is meant especially for people living in the west.

11. Why is it that most major automobile plants are in southern ontario.

12. We'll take the highway leading southeast to regina.

13. That prime minister was better known in the west than in the east.

14. Henry boarded the westbound bus at 1:30 this afternoon.

15. The snow is moving toward the east.

16. The Morgans will be traveling south for the winter.

17. Calgary is located east of vancouver.

18. I've never been as far west as winnipeg.

19. We expect a breeze from the south tonight.

20. Dave will travel east to trois rivières next week.

Other Rules (I)

Languages, Races, Nationalities, and Religions. Capitalize the names of languages, races, nationalities, and religions and the adjectives formed from them.

the Mongolian race	Catholic	Protestant
the Spanish language	Judaism	French
German	Methodist	Italian

Organizations and Institutions. Capitalize important words in the names of organizations, buildings, firms, schools, churches, and other institutions. Do not capitalize *and* or prepositions. Capitalize an article (*a, an,* or *the*) only if it appears as the first word in a name.

Toronto Symphony	Stevens Manufacturing Company
University of Guelph	Uxbridge High School
Church of the Holy Spirit	Canadair
St. Luke's Hospital	Bank of Montreal

Capitalizing Words Correctly. Supply capital letters where needed in these sentences.

1. Some people in switzerland speak french, while others speak german.

2. We took an eastern airlines flight to miami.

3. Dr. Stanley did some research for his book at the public archives.

4. Bill has taken a job with general motors in oshawa.

5. My cousin plans to buy a new buick sedan.

6. Ms. Martin is studying for a degree in japanese art.

7. Do you know the name of our delegate to the united nations?

8. The université laval has an outstanding law school.

9. My aunt has taught at the university of edmonton for many years.

10. Have you bought tickets for the concert given by the toronto symphony orchestra?

11. There was an error in my bill from the bay department store.

12. There has been much fighting in northern ireland between catholics and protestants.

13. The Talmud is a guide to the teachings of judaism.

14. My uncle is very proud of his italian heritage.

15. The people of brazil speak portuguese.

16. Ms. Thompson is a member of the business and professional women's club.

17. He has worked for the lethbridge herald since 1979.

18. Mrs. Smith is a patient in mercy hospital.

19. Tom is traveling to texas on a greyhound bus.

20. Some of my ancestors were french, while some were irish.

Other Rules (II)

Titles of Persons. Capitalize words that show rank, office, or profession, when they are used with a person's name.

Doctor Jones   Senator Parsons   Colonel Bentley
Corporal Thomas   Mayor Grayson   Judge Grant

The titles of high officials are capitalized even when they are used without the official's name.

the Prime Minister of Canada   the Attorney-General   the Mayor

Family Relationships. Capitalize the name of a family relationship when it is used with a person's name.

Aunt Helen   Uncle Dave   Cousin Jim

When words like *mother*, *father*, *dad* and *mom* are used alone in place of a particular person's name, they are capitalized. When modified by a possessive pronoun, as in *your mother*, they are not capitalized. When these and other words of family relationship do not stand for a particular person, they are not capitalized.

We asked Dad to take us fishing.
Sue's dad will prepare the dinner.

Capitalizing Words Correctly. Supply capital letters where needed in the following sentences.

Example: Our family physician is doctor barnes.

1. Do you think your father will be angry with us?

2. The prime minister is flying to europe for a summit conference tomorrow.

3. Did you know that colonel phelps served in the army in germany?

4. The award will be presented by dr. coleman.

5. Next week i'll be visiting my aunt helen and uncle joe.

6. Mr. johnson has an appointment to talk with mayor sims next week.

7. Jim has just been promoted to the rank of sergeant.

8. How long has corporal stuart been in the army?

9. I wish you could have seen dad's face when he heard the news!

10. Meg's mother met the lieutenant-governor yesterday.

11. Henry Kissinger served as secretary of state under presidents nixon and ford.

12. Do you know anyone who has had an audience with the pope?

13. Robert jordan will soon give up his law practice.

14. I gave captain fleming a ride home from the airport.

15. Who is the present prime minister of britain?

Other Rules (III)

Titles of Books and Works of Art. Capitalize the first word and every important word in the titles of books, stories, articles, poems, films, works of art, and musical compositions. The only words considered not important are conjunctions, articles (*a*, *an*, and *the*), and prepositions containing fewer than five letters. But even these are capitalized when used as the first word in a title.

> *Gone with the Wind*   "Back to School"
> *The Call of the Wild*   "Nobody Knows the Trouble I've Seen"

The Deity. Capitalize all words referring to the Deity, the Holy Family, and to religious scriptures.

> God   the Son   the Lord   the Gospel
> the Father   the Holy Spirit   the Bible   the Talmud

Days, Months, Holidays. Capitalize the names of days of the week, of months, and of holidays. Do not capitalize the names of the seasons.

> Thursday   September   Christmas   Thanksgiving   summer   winter

Historical Names. Capitalize the names of historical events, documents and periods.

> World War 1   the Constitution Act   the Middle Ages

Capitalizing Words Correctly. Supply capital letters where needed.

Example: We studied the b̬attle of the b̬ulge in history class.

1. We saw the painting "the last supper" in italy.

2. We will have a thanksgiving holiday.

3. The smiths spend each christmas and two months each summer at their cottage at the lake.

4. There is a buddhist temple in our town.

5. School will be closed on good friday.

6. Chaucer was one of the foremost poets of the middle ages.

7. Sue has three uncles who fought in world war II.

8. The koran is the sacred book of the moslems.

9. Have you read "coming home" by dennis lee?

10. Brother often fought against brother in the american civil war.

11. The talmud is a book of jewish civil and religious laws.

12. We studied the constitution act in our history class.

13. The glee club sang "drink to me only with thine eyes" as their last number.

14. I have one ancestor who fought for the north in the civil war, and one who fought for the south.

15. Margaret atwood wrote the poem called "you refuse to own."

Review: Capitalization

Capitalizing Words Correctly. Supply capital letters where needed in the following sentences.

Example: diane moved to moose jaw, alberta, in november.

1. we studied about homer, the poet from greece, who lived in about 750 b.c.

2. hamlet said, "to be or not to be."

3. have you read any other plays by shakespeare?

4. i hope to visit stratford-on-avon, the poet's birthplace.

5. i asked the receptionist if i was in the right office.

6. she said, "no, you are on the wrong floor."

7. i watched an interview with the famous actor charlie chaplin.

8. the bonds are driving west and will cross the rockies.

9. the traffic on crawford avenue is heavy on saturdays.

10. the french language is melodic when it is spoken well.

11. my mother bought some english china while in london.

12. we walked down main and east on church.

13. we toured the maritimes by greyhound bus.

14. the road leads north to prince albert, saskatchewan, where the carters live.

15. we visited grande prairie last year on our trip out west.

16. the wedding will be held at the fourth presbyterian church.

17. my grandfather was admitted to st. boniface hospital last night.

18. my cousin stan attends northern high school.

19. reverend adams read from the bible during his sunday sermon.

20. the awards were presented by mayor wilson.

21. i'm asking mother right now; go ask your dad.

22. last thanksgiving, aunt helen and uncle jerry visited us.

23. we are reading the poem *vision* by david helwig.

24. i plan to watch *jane eyre* on television tonight.

25. during the depression, many businesses went bankrupt.

Periods and Other End Marks   143

Periods. Place a period at the close of every declarative sentence and of most imperative sentences. A period is also used at the close of groups of words that are used as sentences even though they are not complete sentences.

Please open the window.
I never question your decisions. Never.

Place a period after every part of an abbreviation.

H. G. Wells   Ave.   P.E.I.   P.M.

Exceptions to the rule are certain government agencies and international organizations.

SSC   HWC   DND   RCMP   UN

Question Marks. Place a question mark after an interrogative sentence and after a question that is not a complete sentence.

Can you tell me the date?   Do you know?   When?   Where?

Exclamation Points. Place an exclamation point after an exclamatory sentence and after an exclamation set off from the sentence.

What a sight!   Ouch!   No!   Janie for club president!

Punctuating Sentences. Add periods, question marks, and exclamation points where they are needed in the following sentences.

Example: Our delegate to the UN will address the meeting at 10:30 A.M.

1. What a week we've had
2. Who is the new secretary at the CNIB
3. Don't slam that door
4. What a close call I had
5. Sir John A Macdonald was one of Canada's great Prime Ministers
6. Did you know that many Asians never eat potatoes
7. What a lucky break
8. Mr. F R Elliott has been named chairman of the board of the Stratford Woolen Mills
9. L N Davis, president of Davis Associates, will speak to our club on "Try Again Today"
10. I found out that HWC distributes government publications
11. Wasn't Alexander the Great born in 356 B C
12. The new apartment house at Linden Ave and Third St is ready for occupany
13. What a relief
14. The VA administers benefits to veterans and their dependents
15. Dr A G Lanyon has been our family physician since 1967

Uses of the Comma (I)   144

Introductory Words. Words such as *yes, no, well, why,* and *oh* are followed by a comma:

No, I can't go today.   Why, I forgot all about it!   Oh, I forgot to tell you.

Introductory Phrases and Clauses. These are followed by a comma.

PARTICIPIAL PHRASE   *Crossing the street,* I stumbled and fell.
ADVERBIAL CLAUSE   *When I became tired,* I lay down for a nap.
PREPOSITIONAL PHRASES   *At the back of the house,* we planted a garden.

Transposed Words and Phrases. Words and phrases moved to the beginning of the sentence from their normal position are usually set off by a comma.

Obviously, he'd hate to miss his sister's wedding.

Appositives. An appositive is set off by commas.

Our physician, Dr. Edwards, arrived at ten o'clock.

Using Commas. In the following sentences, insert commas where they belong.

1. Carefully Tom marked his answers on the test booklet.
2. Why I never would have recognized you.
3. Art Graham the new pro at the country club is giving me golf lessons this summer.
4. Although Helen is not an experienced cook she enjoys preparing a meal for guests.
5. At the beginning of the season we knew we would have to work hard to win.
6. Normally I wouldn't have been upset by Dave's question.
7. Smiling amiably Mrs. Olson introduced me to her husband.
8. Well I've done about as much as I can do for one day.
9. To be sure that you've written what you meant to write proofread your paper carefully.
10. Obviously I don't want to miss Dan's graduation.
11. At the top of the pole in front of the post office the flag fluttered.
12. Rising and stretching Bill began to rub his eyes.
13. No I haven't decided what to do.
14. Miss Owens a registered nurse is in charge of first aid at the plant.
15. No I'm afraid I can't attend the conference today.
16. Oh were you hurt?
17. Looking at me suspiciously Mrs. Davis advanced toward me.
18. As I picked up the paper I saw that someone had scribbled on it.
19. Naturally I'll try to be there for the meeting.
20. As I was watching television last night I fell asleep.

Uses of the Comma (II)

Parenthetical Expressions. Words used to explain or qualify a statement are set off by commas. Some common parenthetical expressions are *in fact, I believe, on the other hand, indeed,* and *as a matter of fact.* Conjunctive adverbs used parenthetically are also set off by commas: *moreover, however, consequently,* etc.

> I've decided, *therefore,* to continue my search.
> The decision, *consequently,* is up to you.

Dates and Addresses of More Than One Part. Set off every part after the first from the rest of the sentence.

> ONE PART   Barbara comes from Ontario.
> TWO PARTS   Ajax, Ontario, is her home town.
> THREE PARTS   Her address is 33 Brook Road, Ajax, Ontario K9J 7K5

The day of the month and the month are considered one item: November 14.

Nonrestrictive Clauses and Phrases. These are set off from the rest of the sentence by commas. Restrictive clauses and phrases are not.

> NONRESTRICTIVE   Mary, *wearing a red dress,* walked forward to greet me.
> RESTRICTIVE   The girl *wearing a red dress* is Mary.

Using Commas. Insert commas where they belong in the following sentences. Watch for restrictive clauses and phrases.

> Example: I sent my letter to the company headquarters at 785 Jackson Road, Steinbach, Manitoba R0A 2A0.

1. Indeed I've never questioned your decision.
2. Sue has decided as a matter of fact to study economics.
3. The woman in the blue dress is Mrs. Morton.
4. On March 15 I mailed the package to my cousin in Versailles France.
5. Port Dover which is located on Lake Erie is my old home town.
6. The agency has hired a man who can type and take shorthand.
7. The woman presiding over the meeting is my aunt.
8. Opening the door quickly I saw the presents piled high on the table.
9. The person who has many inner resources is good company for himself or herself.
10. I feel as a matter of fact as if I've never left home.
11. In Montreal Québec Sarah visited the oldest house in the country.
12. My uncle was born on March 21 1930 in Timmins Ontario.
13. On April 10 we flew from Montreal Québec to Houston Texas.
14. The Board has decided moreover to appoint a new head of the company.
15. My raincoat soaked through by the afternoon's downpour was hung up to dry.

Uses of the Comma (III)

Compound Sentences. Place a comma before the conjunction that joins two main clauses in a compound sentence.

> The doctor prescribed some medicine for me, and now I must pick it up at the pharmacy.
> A heavy rain began to fall, but Bill kept on playing golf.

Series. Commas are used to separate the parts of a series. No comma is needed after the last item in a series. Do not use a comma if all parts of the series are joined by *and, or,* or *nor.*

SERIES OF NOUNS	We had our choice of ice cream, cake, or pie.
SERIES OF VERBS	Dave's old car sputtered, shuddered violently, and came to a halt.
SERIES OF PHRASES	We looked for the bracelet under the bed, behind the cushions, and in the dresser drawers.

Using Commas. Insert commas where they belong in the following sentences.

1. Janet graduated on June 9 and on June 10 she began looking for a job.
2. Mother went to three antique shows today—one given by our church one given by a private school and one given at a nearby shopping center.
3. I try to do a good job but it isn't always easy.
4. Martha Bill and Liz were all elected class officers.
5. Sue got to work five minutes early but she found her boss there ahead of her.
6. The furniture in the room consisted of a bed a dresser and a chair.
7. It seems as if I've been dusting sweeping and polishing all day!
8. The lawn mower coughed sputtered and groaned.
9. Won't Helen Meg and Amy come with us?
10. The bus driver hummed cheerfully as he picked up each passenger dropped him off at his destination and then drove to the garage.
11. History math and economics are Sheila's favorite subjects.
12. I paced the floor fiddled with the knobs on the television set and finally sat down.
13. Sue stayed up late last night and now she's exhausted.
14. For dinner we had fried chicken baked potatoes and cole slaw.
15. I don't like to play bridge nor do I like to play backgammon.
16. Soccer hockey and basketball are three of my favorite sports.
17. I've walked jogged and ridden my bicycle all day.
18. Joe sings tenor but Al sings bass.
19. The movie ended and we left the theater hurriedly.
20. I found French easy but German was difficult for me.

Review: End Marks and Commas 147

Punctuating Sentences. Add periods, question marks, and exclamation points where they are needed in the following sentences.

Example: P.T. Barnum originated a traveling circus.

1. What is the temperature outside
2. The class began fifteen minutes late, at 9:15 A M
3. Hooray We have captured the league championship
4. The police are directing traffic at Main St and McCormick Ave
5. I don't like pizza or hamburgers Really
6. Mr J L Kelley is the president of the company
7. Are you willing to spend three dollars to see a movie I'm not
8. Whew I just missed getting hit by a fly ball
9. What in the world is the matter with you
10. Ms Dalbok, our librarian, is shelving the new books now

Using Commas. In the following sentences, insert commas where they belong.

Example: Melanie, our steady babysitter, is going off to college.

1. Indeed I have just completed my assignments.
2. Obviously we could not go in the rain.
3. After I had walked for an hour my feet were aching.
4. Smiling widely the instructor demonstrated the task.
5. Allison our newest little cousin was born last week.
6. Usually I don't eat breakfast in the morning.
7. My sandwich was unfortunately squashed in my locker.
8. We live at 3450 Lakeshore Road Victoria Ontario.
9. There are I believe clean towels in the locker room.
10. The lunch consisted of sloppy joes French fries and cole slaw.
11. The mailman delivered the mail but the check did not arrive.
12. We need to consult books magazines encyclopedias and newspapers for our project.
13. Either sit near the window or sit across the aisle.
14. The corn peas and carrots were overcooked.
15. I did my homework but I did most of it wrong.

The Semicolon

A semicolon is placed between the main clauses of a compound sentence if no conjunction is used.

> Give me the list; I'll check the names. (semicolon in place of *and*)
> Sue will attend the party; she'll be there a little late. (semicolon in place of *but*)

A semicolon is used between main clauses joined by conjunctive adverbs or by phrases like *for example, for instance, in fact.*

> Tom is very tall; *in fact,* he's the tallest boy in our class.

A semicolon is used between main clauses joined by a conjunction if the clause before the conjunction contains commas.

> We visited Kelowna, Kamloops, and Chilliwack; but we still wanted to see more of British Columbia.
> The salesman was friendly, enthusiastic, and persuasive; but still Mrs. Olson hesitated.

A semicolon is used between a series of phrases if they contain commas.

> We have relatives in Markham, Ontario; Montreal, Québec; and Phoenix, Arizona.

Using Semicolons. In the following sentences, replace a comma with a semicolon wherever a semicolon is needed.

> Example: Come visit me when you can; I'm always glad to see you.

1. I'm exhausted, I've been playing tennis all day.

2. Sue's favorite subject is French, in fact, she often reads French novels in her free time.

3. Dave takes math, English, Canadian history, and chemistry, but his favorite subject is history.

4. Last summer the Smiths visited Vienna, Austria, Budapest, Hungary, and Munich, Germany.

5. Sally has attended schools in England, France, and the United States, but she likes our school best.

6. Martha won the scholarship, furthermore, she is eligible for financial aid as well.

7. For lunch we had cheeseburgers, potato salad, and cole slaw, but we were still hungry enough to eat sundaes for dessert.

8. Mr. Burns arrived late for the meeting, consequently, he heard nothing of the speeches.

9. Mr. Emery collects stamps, moreover, he's also a coin collector.

10. We took our vacation in April, as a result, we'll be staying home the rest of the year.

The Colon

A colon is used to introduce a list of items. Often it is preceded by the words *the following*, or *as follows*. The colon is not used before a series of modifiers or complements immediately following the verb.

> We have visited the following countries: Germany, France, Holland, and Switzerland.
> The girls in the play were Helen, Nancy, and Betty. (series of complements)

A colon is used to introduce a formal quotation.

> The Prime Minister began his speech by saying: "We must decide how best to work with our Allies."

A colon is used between two sentences when the second explains the first. The second sentence begins with a capital letter.

> James Jordan smiled happily: He had just been elected Mayor.

A colon is also used (1) after the formal salutation of a letter, (2) between hour and minute figures of clock time, (3) in Biblical references, (4) between the title and subtitle of a book, (5) between numbers referring to volume and pages of books and magazines.

> Gentlemen: 1:30 P.M.   Exodus 20:3   *Captain Caution: A Chronicle of Arundel*   Volume III: page 68

Using Colons. Place a colon wherever it is needed below.

1. Our plane leaves at 8 30 A.M. tomorrow.
2. Have you read *The Late George Apley A Novel in the Form of a Memoir?*
3. Next fall Betty will take the following subjects French, physics, history, and English.
4. I found the answer to my question in Volume IV page 38.
5. The minister read from John 20 1-18 this morning.
6. Bill will take French, physics, history, and English next fall.
7. Some of Mark's favorite cities are the following Vancouver, St. John's, and Toronto.
8. Mr. Black ended his speech with a quotation from Martin Luther "It makes a difference whose ox is gored."
9. To apply for the job you will need to supply the following a summary of the schools you've attended, a list of your previous jobs, and the names of three references.
10. Helen is interested in the following professions medicine, dentistry, and law.
11. Please send the following boys to the principal's office Tim Jacobson, Dan Phelps, and John Osborn.
12. The mayor ended her speech with a quotation from Aesop "Familiarity breeds contempt."

The Dash and Parentheses

A dash is used to show a break or interruption in thought, or after a series to indicate a summarizing statement.

> The day—a hectic but pleasant one—was finally over.
> Her necklaces, her bracelets, her earrings—all the old woman's treasures were on display.

Parentheses are used to enclose supplementary or explanatory words. Usually the material enclosed by parentheses is so loosely related to the main thought that it might be better rewritten as a separate sentence.

> Dick (not Tom) was elected president of the club.
> I have a feeling (don't you?) that Ann will get the part in the play.

Using the Dash and Parentheses. Rewrite the following sentences, inserting dashes or parentheses where they are needed.

> Example: I know you'd find Uncle Arthur amusing(but that's another story).

1. The speaker's effect on his listeners most of them tired to begin with was to put them to sleep.

2. Stop that racket I mean that noise!

3. The sightseeing, the living out of a suitcase, the awareness of new ways of living all this was over for another year.

4. I'm sure aren't you? that Marcia will get the job.

5. The week's work exhausting but enjoyable gave George a feeling of accomplishment.

6. Skim milk not whole milk is on Marcia's diet.

7. Books, radio, television all these kept Tom busy while he was in the hospital.

8. Dick Johnson a popular but very modest boy is our club president.

9. New Brunswick, Nova Scotia, Prince Edward Island all these provinces help make the Maritimes my favorite section of the country.

10. After I had my tonsils out, ice cream not solid food tasted good to me.

Review: The Semicolon, the Colon, the Dash, and Parentheses

Using Semicolons. In the following sentences, replace a comma with a semicolon wherever a semicolon is needed.

Example: The telephone message was urgent, I was to call immediately.

1. The chicken was cooked to perfection, it was crisp and tasty.
2. I enjoy reading mysteries, for instance, the *Nancy Drew* series is good.
3. The contestants came from Gander, Newfoundland, Antigonish, Nova Scotia, and Nanaimo, British Columbia.
4. We dusted, scrubbed, mopped, and swept, but still the house looked a mess.
5. The days are getting shorter, soon it will be winter.

Using the Colon. Place a colon where it belongs in each sentence below.

Example: I have worked as the following:bus boy, waiter, clerk, and stock boy.

1. The visiting schedule is as follows parents on Monday, friends on Tuesday.
2. The letter was begun with "Dear Sirs", but a woman received it.
3. Jeremy went to bed early He was exhausted from his jogging.
4. The teacher recommended *Breaking the Sound Barrier A Phonics Handbook*.
5. The bus leaves at 12 30 and every half hour thereafter.

Using the Dash and Parentheses. In the following sentences, insert dashes or parentheses where they are needed.

Example: The field trip more interesting than we had expected lasted all day.

1. I have a feeling I hope I am mistaken that something is wrong at home.

2. The director not the actors came out to take a bow after the play.

3. Heavy foods not fruits and vegetables contribute to high cholesterol.

4. The marigolds, the zinnias, the sweet peas all were in bloom.

5. My mother told me and I will never forget it that it is always best to tell the truth.

The Possessive of Nouns (I)

The **apostrophe** is used with nouns to show possession or ownership. The possessive form of a singular noun is usually made by adding an apostrophe and s ('s).

Don—Don's dog   girl—girl's book

The possessive of plural nouns is formed by adding an apostrophe and s ('s). However, if the plural noun ends in s, add only the apostrophe to form the possessive.

women—women's hats   birds—birds' cages
salesmen—salesmen's orders   books—books' covers

Using Apostrophes Correctly. For each of the following sentences, write the correct possessive form of the italicized noun.

Example: The four *witnesses* testimony all differed. _witnesses'_

1. The *boys* accounts of their trip were all different. _____

2. *Tom* horse won the race. _____

3. *The Premier will address the mayors* conference. _____

4. The *ladies* hats and coats were all placed in the cloakroom. _____

5. The *debaters* meeting will be held at four o'clock. _____

6. The *men* shoes in that store are all imported from Italy. _____

7. Local newspapermen are attending an *editors* conference in Toronto. _____

8. The *cities* problems are well known. _____

9. The *toys* safety features have been discussed. _____

10. The *sopranos* duet was well received. _____

11. The *enemies* armies have been defeated. _____

12. The *children* playground is a block from here. _____

13. The *students* questionnaires have all been returned. _____

14. My *sister* math book has been lost. _____

15. Haven't the *actors* parts been difficult to learn? _____

16. The soldier received a *hero* welcome. _____

17. The *judge* decision was a surprise. _____

18. *Jane* house is the third one from the corner. _____

19. The *waiter* tips for the day amounted to a large sum. _____

20. We inspected all the *animals* cages at the zoo. _____

The Possessive of Nouns (II)

A **compound noun** is a noun composed of more than one word. Only the last part of a compound noun shows possession.

father-in-law's car   editor-in-chief's job

When two or more nouns are used to show joint ownership, only the last noun mentioned is given the possessive form. The rule also applies to firm names and to names of organizations.

Susan and Amy's church   National Food Store's policy

If the nouns are used to show separate ownership, each name is given the possessive form.

Helen's and Margaret's houses   Jack's and Ken's jackets

Use an apostrophe and *s* to form the possessive of indefinite pronouns: *one's* boat, *someone else's* house. Never use an apostrophe to form the possessive of personal pronouns: *ours, yours, his, hers, its, theirs.*

Using Apostrophes Correctly. For the following sentences, write the correct possessive form of the italicized words.

Example: The *robins* and *sparrows* nests were empty. ___*robins'*___
___*sparrows'*___

1. I stopped the car in front of *Ellen* and *Mary* school. _____
2. The dog is wagging *its* tail. _____
3. Isn't that jacket *yours*? _____
4. Tom dented the fender of his *mother-in-law* car. _____
5. That must be *someone else* book. _____
6. *Helen* and *Jane* names appeared on the library card. _____
7. What is the *University Womens Club* membership policy? _____
8. Our poor harvest from the vegetable garden is *nobody* fault. _____
9. The Whitmans turned in their tickets, but we had lost *ours*. _____
10. The *Morgans* and *Swansons* cars were damaged in the collision. ___

11. Stuart is driving the *commander-in-chief* car. _____
12. I always wash my sweaters, but Jill has *hers* dry-cleaned. _____
13. *Nobody* golf game is perfect. _____
14. That money is *his*. _____
15. What are the *editor-in-chief* duties? _____
16. Have you been to *Simpson Sears* sale? _____
17. The victory is *theirs*. _____
18. Have you seen *Johns* ad? _____
19. *Zehrs* check-cashing policy is fair. _____
20. *Edna* and *Rod* house was damaged by fire. _____

Other Uses for the Apostrophe   154

When used as adjectives, words expressing time and amount are given the possessive form.

> an hour's pay   three months' wait   two months' work

An apostrophe is used to show the omission of letters or figures.

> class of '83 (1983)   couldn't (could not)   we're (we are)

An apostrophe is also used to show the plurals of letters, words, numbers, and signs. (In print, such expressions are *italicized*. In manuscript, they may be underlined or placed in quotation marks.)

> How many *s's* are in your name?
> He used too many *if's* in his talk.
> Saddle shoes were popular in the 1940's.

Using Apostrophes Correctly. Write the correct possessive or plural form of the italicized word in each sentence below.

Example: I lost a *day* pay when I was sick. ___*day's*___

1. There will be three *months* delay in the construction of the building.
   _____
2. It is now three *oclock*. _____
3. Your *2s* look like *3s*. _____
4. Mrs. Smith graduated from college with the class of *58*. _____
5. *Doesnt* your dog want to come in? _____
6. Jim bought a *dollar* worth of gas last night. _____
7. Ms. Hansen gets three *weeks* vacation. _____
8. Be sure you dot your *is* in your papers. _____
9. The Olson family had gone to the World's Fair of *64*. _____
10. *Were* always eager to see you. _____
11. Sheila was promised two *months* work. _____
12. Seven *years* study is needed if you want to become a lawyer. _____
13. Jane's house is just ten *minutes* walk from mine. _____
14. You *mustnt* worry about it. _____
15. There are three *sos* in your sentence. _____
16. The mountains are only forty *minutes* ride from here. _____
17. *Well* be in the city in an *hour* time. _____
18. The past *year* history has been full of surprises. _____
19. The little boy bought five *cents* worth of candy. _____
20. When we thanked the fireman, he said it was all in a *day* work. _____

Review: The Apostrophe

Using Apostrophes Correctly. For each of the following sentences, write the correct possessive form of the italicized noun.

Example: The *dignitaries* seats were all reserved. *dignitaries'*

1. The *typewriter* ribbon needs changing. _____
2. None of the *children* books were returned to the library. _____
3. The *men* locker room is overcrowded. _____
4. This *theater* movies are always first run. _____
5. The weeping *willow* roots were interfering with the sewer. _____
6. The *dresses* colors faded in the bright sun. _____
7. It is the *editor-in-chief* job to proofread all articles. _____
8. Have you ever met *Bonnie and Allen* parents? _____
9. We recommended that they buy a lawn mower like *ours*. _____
10. One should always take good care of *one* teeth. _____
11. The teacher was impressed with *David* and *Matt* work. _____
12. We like to buy that *dairy* milk because it is fresh daily. _____
13. The *officer-in-command* vehicle is parked in front. _____
14. We responded to *Baskin and Robbins* ad for help wanted. _____
15. The *Audi* and *Mercedes* front ends look similar. _____

Using Apostrophes Correctly. Rewrite each of the following sentences. Insert apostrophes where needed.

Example: The little boy could not say his *ss*.

The little boy could not say his s's.

1. Who was the valedictorian of the class of 77?

_____

2. I couldn't follow his argument because of all the *ifs*, *ands*, and *buts*.

_____

3. The construction crew finished the job in three weeks time.

_____

4. At camp, the days activities are all mapped out.

_____

5. The Hustle will be known as the dance of the 70s.

_____

Direct Quotations

Quotation marks are used to enclose a *direct quotation*. In a direct quotation, the words of the speaker are directly quoted exactly as he or she spoke them.

Quotation marks are never used with an indirect quotation, which reports the meaning of the speaker but not the exact words.

INDIRECT	Jim said that he would like to play tennis.
DIRECT	Jim said, "I would like to play tennis."
INDIRECT	The woman asked Dave if he needed a job.
DIRECT	"Do you need a job?" the woman asked Dave.

Identifying Direct Quotations. Read each sentence below. If it is a direct quotation and requires quotation marks, write **D** in the blank. If the sentence is an indirect quotation, write **I** in the blank.

Example: I bought a new dress, said Mary. ____*D*

1. Alice said, You look all tired out. _____

2. The teacher asked us to be quiet. _____

3. I will introduce the speaker, said Tom. _____

4. The president asked the secretary to read the minutes of the last meeting. _____

5. Mrs. Keith asked, Do you think summer will ever come? _____

6. The teacher asked if we understood the assignment. _____

7. Do you want to go to the movies? asked Ken. _____

8. What kind of work do you do, asked Mrs. Smith. _____

9. Bill said that he had already studied his French assignment. _____

10. The sermon will be on the subject of forgiveness, said the minister.

_____

11. Five weeks is too long to live out of a suitcase, the girl replied. _____

12. The policeman asked if we were lost. _____

13. I've never played chess before, admitted George. _____

14. Don't go near the water, Mother said. _____

15. What is your favorite novel? asked Susan. _____

16. Ms. Turner said that we should turn in our notebooks. _____

17. The only thing we have to fear is fear itself, said President Roosevelt.

_____

18. Let's go for a walk, suggested Peter. _____

19. Who is to blame for this? asked Dan. _____

20. I've never been so tired in my life, said Don. _____

Writing Direct Quotations

In dialogue, the first word of the quotation is capitalized. The speaker's words are set off from the rest of the sentence by a comma. When the end of the quotation is also the end of the sentence, the end punctuation falls inside the quotation marks.

>Marian said, "I've seen that movie three times."

If the quoted words are a question or exclamation, the end punctuation falls inside the quotation marks unless the whole sentence is a question or exclamation.

>"Ouch! I burned my finger!" Susan cried.
>Did Bob say, "It's my fault"?

Material quoted may begin in the middle of a sentence; if so, the first word is not capitalized. At the close of a quotation, a colon or semicolon falls inside the quotation marks.

>Mary said, "One can live graciously only in a city"; I don't agree.

Both parts of a divided quotation are enclosed in quotes, but the second part is not capitalized unless it is a new sentence. A new paragraph and new quotation marks show a change in speaker.

>"The mayor's speech was wonderful," said Mrs. Brown. "We enjoyed it."
>"But," said her husband, "hadn't you heard it all before?"

Writing Quotations Correctly. Read each sentence below. Insert the proper punctuation.

Example: "What time did you get up this morning?" asked Tim.

1. What salary asked Ms. Means do you require

2. I've never known said Mr. Ogden just how to take his jokes.

3. You can't be serious exclaimed Kate.

4. I can now plan said Miss Black for next week's work.

5. We can plan ahead now Mrs. Martin said what should we do next week

6. I'll take the blame for that Dan said.

7. I don't believe a word of it shouted Ken.

8. I will not allow anyone said the policeman to leave the premises.

9. Bob admitted I don't really understand that problem.

10. I don't know what I'd do said Mr. Grady without my calculator.

11. Let's play Monopoly Kim suggested it's such a good game.

12. I won't take the responsibility for that exclaimed Pat.

13. Don't you ever get tired of listening to the radio asked Mother.

14. I'm sure said Martha that I should be saving more money.

15. Did Ellen say it's too hot to play tennis

Quotations within Quotations. Single quotation marks are used to enclose a quotation within a quotation.

> "The sign said, 'Deposit all litter in trash barrel,' " Mother pointed out.
> Tom said, "I'm glad Bill told me, 'I agree completely.' "

Setting Off Titles. Use quotation marks to enclose the titles of chapters, stories, poems, essays, articles and songs.

> You'd like James Plunkett's short story "The Half-Crown."
> "Youth and Age" is a poem by the Irish writer, Eleanor Hull.

Words Used in Special Ways. Words used in special ways are enclosed in quotation marks.

> Ben calls the people of our town the "locals."

A word referred to as a word is put in italics.

> The word *ingress* means "entrance."

Using Quotations Correctly. Insert the appropriate punctuation in each of the following sentences.

> Example: "The Boy Scouts' motto is 'Be prepared,' said Dave.

1. Have you read O. Henry's short story The Whirligig of Life
2. Jim told me You and I will never get rich said Martha.
3. The word *dollop* means a lump or a large hunk.
4. I know you'd like Margaret Avison's poem Watershed.
5. Bill said After that she told me Look who's talking.
6. Have you read David Helwig's poem Vision
7. Jim claimed that his new car was a real beauty.
8. Do you know the song Get Me to the Church on Time asked Peg.
9. The instructions say Wash in hot water Sue explained.
10. Did you know that the word *tenable* means capable of being held or defended Jean asked.
11. To Build a Fire is the name of a good short story by Jack London.
12. Al asked Are you sure that Pete said That's not my job
13. I dislike the expression Have a good day.
14. There are several stories I'd recommend, such as Lilacs.
15. In the book *The Asians* I was especially interested in the chapter The Japanese Woman and the chapter Politics in Japan.
16. Let me read you Eli Mandel's poem Song.
17. Didn't the sign say Trenton — 10 kilometres asked Mother.
18. Have you read the chapter The Impact of the West in the book *The Arabs in History*?
19. Didn't the restaurant's ad say Open at Five O'clock Martha asked.
20. Al said I like to read novels by Rex Stout answered Meg.

Identifying Direct Quotations. Read each sentence below. If it is a direct quotation and requires quotation marks, write **D** in the blank. If the sentence is an indirect quotation, write **I** in the blank.

Example: There's a fly in my soup, complained the patron. _*D*_

1. Jerry said he was tired and wanted to rest. _____
2. Help yourself to the fruit, said Mother. _____
3. We asked the neighbors to take in our mail during our vacation. _____
4. Gladly! they responded. _____
5. The announcer said, And now time out for a station break. _____

Writing Quotations Correctly. Read each sentence below. Insert the proper punctuation where needed.

Example: Gail asked, "How can you eat strawberries without sugar?"

1. Wow! said the little boy, I have never seen so many cars.
2. You will find, said the salesman, that this is our finest model.
3. The ad said that there was a sale on sheets and towels.
4. I wonder how much they cost? said Ellen.
5. Did Mike say, I can't come tomorrow?
6. The babysitter asked, When do I have to change his diaper?
7. Somehow, pondered the deliveryman, I have to get this up three flights of stairs.
8. The clock must have stopped, observed Sue. Do you know what time it is?
9. Watch out, warned the foreman. The wires are loose!
10. Who is responsible for this accident? questioned the policeman.

Using Quotations Correctly. Insert the appropriate punctuation in each of the following sentences.

Example: The social worker said, "This report is marked 'Confidential.'"

1. I like the poem Annabel Lee by Edgar Allan Poe.
2. The sign warns No Trespassing, exclaimed Valerie.
3. I don't like people who call us teeny-boppers.
4. Why did Dad say Get to bed? wondered Carl.
5. The word *egress* means exit.

The Final Silent e

When a suffix beginning with a vowel is added to a word ending in a silent *e*, the *e* is usually dropped.

take—taking   admire—admiration
fame—famous   fascinate—fascination

When the final silent *e* is preceded by *c* or *g*, the *e* is usually retained before a suffix beginning with *a* or *o*.

notice—noticeable   service—serviceable

When a suffix beginning with a consonant is added to a word ending in silent *e*, the *e* is usually retained.

same—sameness   improve—improvement
EXCEPTIONS   truly, argument, wholly, awful

Adding Suffixes to Words Ending in Silent e. In each sentence below, change the italicized word to the correct form. Choose from these suffixes: *-ing, -al, -ion, -ation, -able, -ous, -ful, -less, -ly, -ment*

Example: The boys gave an *amaze* performance on the trampoline.

_____ *amazing* _____

1. He has not received much formal *educate*. _____
2. Did you have an *appraise* of the value of your house? _____
3. What are the grocery stores *charge* for cantaloupe now? _____
4. The old man is often *care* about his clothes. _____
5. They are thinking of *name* the baby Cara. _____
6. Dick Mason found himself *fame* overnight. _____
7. Mr. Morgan has many *admire* qualities. _____
8. Whether Jack should take that job is *debate*. _____
9. Tom is *change* rapidly as he grows older. _____
10. Tony is *grease* the pan before he makes the cake. _____
11. To Beth's *amaze*, she won first prize. _____
12. The lecturer is *wide* known throughout the province. _____
13. Jean and Sue have never had an *argue*. _____
14. We all have much *admire* for Terry Fox. _____
15. Have you studied the *Constitute* Act? _____
16. Miss Hanson is very *waste* in her cooking. _____
17. He made a *courage* attempt to rescue the little girl. _____
18. Tim seems to be caught in a *hope* situation. _____
19. Mrs. Harris is *give* a great deal to charity this year. _____
20. What *architecture* features of the building do you like? _____

Words Ending in y

When a suffix is added to a word ending in *y* preceded by a consonant, **the *y* is usually changed to *i*.**

There are two exceptions: (1) when *-ing* is added, the *y* does **not** change; (2) some one-syllable words do not change the *y*, as *dryness, shyness.*

hazy—haziness	envy—envying
cherry—cherries	penny—pennies
marry—married	merry—merriment

When a suffix is added to a word ending in *y* preceded by a vowel, **the *y* usually does not change.**

say—saying	employ—employer
joy—joyful	delay—delayed

EXCEPTIONS   daily, gaily

Adding Suffixes to Words Ending in *y*. In each sentence below, change the italicized word to the correct form. Choose from these suffixes: *-ness, -es, -ed, -age, -ing, -able, -er, -ful, -est, -ly*

Example: Tom and Ellen were *marry* June 20. _*married*_

1. The children are *play* with their new toys. _____

2. They are *relay* that information via satellite. _____

3. The aviator's homecoming was a *joy* occasion. _____

4. Ed reads the *funny* before he reads anything else. _____

5. Loren has just *carry* my groceries into the house. _____

6. The *dry* of the soil was evident. _____

7. The little boy bought candy with his five *penny*. _____

8. The pirate has *bury* his gold. _____

9. Mr. Todd's hair is *gray* than Mr. Smith's. _____

10. Kate outgrew her *shy* as she grew older. _____

11. We are *delay* our return until Monday. _____

12. The *busy* of the market place astounded her. _____

13. Mrs. Owens went on her *day* rounds as if nothing had happened. _____

14. Jim has been *employ* at the post office for two years. _____

15. The little girl danced *gay* into the room. _____

16. We have *enjoy* our stay in Florida. _____

17. Mr. Beard is *copy* the recipe. _____

18. Sheila left the room *hasty*. _____

19. Dave is not *worry* about the future. _____

20. The moving men picked up the refrigerator *easy*. _____

Prefixes and Suffixes

The Suffixes -ness and -ly. When the suffix -ly is added to a word ending in l, both l's are retained. When -ness is added to a word ending in n, both n's are retained.

actual—actually   even—evenness
gradual—gradually   thin—thinness

The Addition of Prefixes. When a prefix is added to a word, the spelling of the word remains the same.

disappear   presoak   transaction   misstep
improve   rezone   cooperate   irrelevant

Words with the "Seed" Sound. Only one English word ends in sede: supersede. Three other words end in ceed: exceed, proceed, succeed. All other words ending in the "seed" sound are spelled cede: secede, recede, concede, accede, precede.

Correcting Spelling Errors. Underline the spelling error in each of the following sentences. Write the correct spelling of each underlined word in the blank after each sentence.

Example: We <u>gradualy</u> increased our speed. ___*gradually*___

1. Tom seems shy, but he actually is quite outgoing. _____

2. Don will sesede from membership in this club. _____

3. The eveness of the two teams is obvious. _____

4. The candidate conseded defeat. _____

5. The thiness of the ice made skating dangerous. _____

6. We carefuly went down the steep steps. _____

7. New methods of mining have superceded old ones. _____

8. The flood waters have finally begun to receed. _____

9. We have gradualy added to the size of our farm. _____

10. Tim has increased the size of his account substantialy. _____

11. Be sure to dress casualy for the picnic. _____

12. Does Ontario's production of corn excede Manitoba's? _____

13. I acede to your proposal. _____

14. The cleaness of the hotel room was noticeable. _____

15. Ms. Thomas has certainly suceeded in her profession. _____

16. The dignitaries will now procede to the platform. _____

17. Mrs. Brown preceeded us as we entered the restaurant. _____

18. Didn't he look at you evily? _____

19. Monique is realy quite industrious. _____

20. Idealy, we should all be as happy as kings. _____

Words with *ie* and *ei*

When the sound is long *e* (ē), the word is spelled *ie* except after *c*.

I BEFORE E

piece   priest   brief   yield   chief

EXCEPT AFTER C

perceive   ceiling   conceive   deceit   receipt

EXCEPTIONS TO THE RULE

either   neither   financier   weird   species   seize   leisure

Correcting Spelling Errors. Underline the misspelled word in each sentence below. Write the word correctly in the blank.

Example: What is your <u>beleif</u> about the treaty? ___*belief*___

1. Can iether John or Jim solve the puzzle? _____

2. Mrs. Todd plays bridge in her liesure time. _____

3. Ms. Norman painted the cieling of the kitchen yesterday. _____

4. Breifly, here are my plans for the week. _____

5. The broker spoke about the interest currently yeilded by government

bonds. _____

6. Mrs. Hansen's neice is visiting her this week. _____

7. I was issued a reciept for my purchase. _____

8. Have a peice of cake, Eleanor. _____

9. I can't concieve of a nicer homecoming. _____

10. The preist walked into the cathedral. _____

11. Who is the present cheif of police in Collingwood? _____

12. Niether Mary nor Ann knows how to play chess. _____

13. The warrior's sheild bore his coat of arms. _____

14. His message was full of trickery and deciet. _____

15. The financeir is used to dealing with huge sums of money. _____

16. Sieze every opportunity to improve yourself! _____

17. What speceis of moth is that? _____

18. The children dressed in wierd costumes on Hallowe'en. _____

19. I was much releived at the outcome of the tests. _____

20. Mr. Ray beleives that this is the best of all possible times. _____

Doubling the Final Consonant

In one-syllable words ending in one consonant preceded by one vowel, double the final consonant before adding a suffix beginning with a vowel.

sit—sitting	slug—slugged	plan—planning
brag—bragged	big—biggest	tan—tanner

The final consonant is doubled in words of more than one syllable when the word ends in one consonant preceded by one vowel, *and* the word is accented on the last syllable.

omit'—omitted	refer'—referred
submit'—submitted	begin'—beginning

However, if the newly formed word is accented on a different syllable, the final consonant is not doubled.

confer'—conference   refer'—reference

Correcting Spelling Errors. Underline the misspelled word in each sentence below. Write the word correctly in the blank.

Example: I <u>omited</u> my signature on the letter. *omitted*

1. We have been siting still for three hours. _____

2. What is your preferrence in television programs? _____

3. Al's name was omited from the list of speakers. _____

4. Mr. Olson was braging about his many trips to Europe. _____

5. I've checked every referrence book in the library! _____

6. Your house is biger than mine. _____

7. I never refered to the atlas when I did my research. _____

8. Mrs. Miller is a member of the planing commission. _____

9. I submited my letter of resignation to the board. _____

10. When I was in Europe, I prefered Italy to France. _____

11. What's the diferrence between ice cream and sherbet? _____

12. Don braged about his new car. _____

13. Mr. Hunter is a beginer in photography. _____

14. How much of your salary have you alloted to rent? _____

15. I am defering to your judgment. _____

16. You are forgeting that you owe me a letter! _____

17. She defered paying the phone bill last month. _____

18. July was hoter than June. _____

19. Mr. Tilden has been siting on the porch all day. _____

20. The news was upseting to me. _____

Words Often Confused (I)

Some words sound alike but are spelled differently and have different meanings. For example: *hear*, meaning to listen to, and *here*, meaning at this place. *Hear* and *here* are homonyms. Here is a list of homonyms and other words often confused. Study the spelling and meaning of each.

aid means to help, support, or assist.
aide means any official assistant.
desert means a wilderness or dry, sandy region with sparse vegetation.
desert means to abandon.
dessert (note the change in spelling) is a sweet such as cake or pie.
hear means to listen to, or take notice of.
here means in this place.
lose means to mislay or suffer the loss of something.
loose means free or not fastened.

Choosing the Correct Spelling. In each sentence below, underline the correct spelling of the word that properly belongs in the sentence.

Example: We had apple pie for (desert, <u>dessert</u>).

1. The nurse's (aid, aide) took the patient's temperature.
2. How many people have crossed the Sahara (Desert, Dessert)?
3. A button on my jacket came (lose, loose).
4. (Hear, Here) are the seashells I promised you.
5. Proceeds from the sale will be used in (aid, aide) of the hospital expansion program.
6. The mother bear will never (desert, dessert) her cubs.
7. Did you (hear, here) the announcement over the loudspeaker?
8. I don't want to (lose, loose) my only contact with you.
9. An (aid, aide) accompanied the Premier to the conference.
10. After a big dinner we had a light sherbet for (desert, dessert).
11. The seat of my little brother's tricycle is (lose, loose).
12. Put your books (hear, here).
13. Don't (lose, loose) your notebook.
14. Did you (hear, here) the doorbell?
15. I won't ever (lose, loose) my respect for Mr. Allison.
16. The Humane Society needs voluteer (aid, aide) on Tag Day.
17. I'm sure his friends will never (desert, dessert) him.
18. The label is (lose, loose) on my jacket.
19. (Hear, Here) are the directions to follow.
20. The clasp is (lose, loose) on my necklace.

Words Often Confused (II)

Here is another list of words often confused.

its is a word that indicates ownership.
it's is a contraction for *it is* or *it has*.

principal describes something or someone of chief or central importance.
principle is a basic truth, standard, or rule of behavior.

stationary means fixed or unmoving.
stationery refers to paper and envelopes used for writing letters.

there means in that place.
their means belonging to them.
they're is a contraction for *they are*.

to means toward, or in the direction of.
too means also or very.
two is the number 2.

weather refers to atmospheric conditions such as temperature or cloudiness.
whether helps express choice or alternative.

whose is the possessive form of who.
who's is a contraction for *who is* or *who has*.

your is the possessive form of *you*.
you're is a contraction for *you are*.

Choosing the Correct Spelling. In each sentence below, underline the correct spelling of the word that properly belongs in the sentence.

1. The bird is in (its, it's) cage.
2. (Whose, Who's) to blame for the misunderstanding?
3. What is the (weather, whether) forecast for tomorrow?
4. The (principal, principle) of our school is Mr. Holmes.
5. I learned the (principals, principles) of chess two years ago.
6. We use a (stationary, stationery) bicycle for exercise in bad weather.
7. Mr. Sawyer is the (principal, principle) stockholder in the corporation.
8. (Its, It's) never too late to make an apology.
9. It's not the money; it's the (principal, principle) of the thing!
10. You must make your own decision; (its, it's) completely up to you.
11. Our dog has lost (its, it's) collar.
12. Sue doesn't know (weather, whether) to take French or German.
13. Have you ordered (your, you're) pizza yet?
14. (There, Their, There are) apt to be some risks in the venture.
15. What is the (principal, principle) lesson you've learned from all this?
16. The Olsons have sold (there, their, they're) house.
17. I replied to the invitation on my new white (stationary, stationery).
18. Is that (your, you're) boat?
19. (There, Their, They're) interested in buying a new car.
20. (Its, It's) a hard decision to make.

Spelling Words with Added Suffixes. In each sentence below, change the italicized word to the correct form by adding a suffix. Choose from these suffixes: *-ing, -al, -ion, -able, -ous, -ful, -less, -ly, -ation, -ness, -es, -ed, -age, -ing, -able, -er, -ful, -ment.*

Example: John is the most *boast* boy in class. _____*boastful*_____

1. The doctor noticed an *improve* in his patient's condition. _____
2. The children showed *admire* for their parents. _____
3. Dad is going into *retire* at the end of the year. _____
4. How much are they *charge* for those wheel covers? _____
5. Cheryl is *hope* to become a veterinarian. _____
6. Our *happy* was spoiled by the death of our pet. _____
7. We were *delay* by a huge traffic jam. _____
8. The child picked all the *blueberry* out of the muffin. _____
9. Why are you *hurry* if class doesn't start for ten minutes? _____
10. We worked *busy* late into the night. _____

Correcting Spelling Errors. Underline the spelling error in each of the following sentences. Write the correct spelling of each underlined word on the blank.

Example: The stock boy is <u>carring</u> our packages to the car. *Carrying*

1. This owner's manual is very <u>helpfull</u>. _____
2. I am <u>celebrateing</u> my birthday today. _____
3. Tomorrow is <u>actualy</u> my birthday. _____
4. How could you <u>mispell</u> such a simple word? _____
5. The <u>marryage</u> is taking place at noon. _____
6. Bill is considered an <u>iresponsible</u> boy. _____
7. Our problem is <u>largly</u> one of lack of funds. _____
8. I have not <u>recieved</u> any gifts for graduation. _____
9. What a <u>releif</u> that the temperature is down. _____
10. We are <u>planing</u> to have a barbecue over the weekend. _____
11. Have you seen the <u>begining</u> of this movie? _____
12. The dog broke <u>lose</u> from his chain. _____
13. <u>Its</u> raining outside, so we will remain indoors. _____
14. The workers left <u>there</u> tools behind. _____
15. I wonder <u>weather</u> there is a mistake in this sentence. _____

Plurals Formed with *s* and *es*

The plural of most nouns is formed by adding *s*. The plural of nouns ending in *s*, *sh*, *ch*, *x*, and *z* is formed by adding *es*.

cat—cats   brush—brushes

Spelling Plurals Correctly. In each of the following sentences, change the singular noun given in parentheses into the plural form. Write it in the blank.

Example: There are three (church) in our town. _Churches_

1. How many (employee) does the Watson Company have? _____

2. Please close all the (window). _____

3. We cut two large (branch) from the tree. _____

4. Three (day) from now, we will be in Hull. _____

5. The judges' (badge) bore their names. _____

6. We had five (test) in history last term. _____

7. All the mothers tied the (sash) of their daughters' dresses. _____

8. We were startled when the dog sprang at us from the (bush). _____

9. After painting, we cleaned our (brush). _____

10. How many (bus) go to Burlington each day? _____

11. The woodsmen sharpened their (axe). _____

12. Please fill the Christmas (box) with the toys. _____

13. How many of the (sense) are mentioned in that paragraph? _____

14. There are forty (girl) in the glee club. _____

15. Ms. Mason and Mr. Gibbs are (teacher) at the school. _____

16. Uncle Martin and Aunt Peg exchanged (kiss). _____

17. How many varieties of (glass) are there? _____

18. The new secretary has three (boss). _____

19. We have bought and sold three (house) in the last five years. _____

20. Sam and Barb packed (lunch) for the picnic. _____

21. How many (box) of candy did you order? _____

22. Mr. Thomas can speak seven (language). _____

23. What are your favorite (magazine)? _____

24. Needlepoint is one of the (class) offered by the Y. W. C. A. _____

25. I have not reported my (loss) to the police. _____

Nouns Ending in y

When a noun ends in *y* preceded by a consonant, the plural is formed by changing *y* to *i* and adding *es*.

        company—companies   worry—worries   beauty—beauties

When a noun ends in *y* preceded by a vowel, the plural is formed by adding *s*.

        play—plays   valley—valleys   delay—delays

Spelling Plurals Correctly. In each of the following sentences, change the singular noun given in parentheses into the plural form. Write it in the blank.

        Example: Ann has appeared in three (play) this year. _*plays*_

1. There are eleven (boy) in the kindergarten class. _____

2. Those (toy) were all imported from Germany. _____

3. In Russia those writers are considered (enemy) of the state. _____

4. Dan has few (worry) about the future. _____

5. Let's have some (cherry) and grapes for dessert. _____

6. There have been many (delay) in the shipments. _____

7. What steel (company) were established in the '20's? _____

8. The new colts were little (beauty). _____

9. There are (valley) between those ranges of hills. _____

10. How many (holiday) are there between New Year's Day and the First of July? _____

11. There are twelve (caddy) on duty at Twin Oaks Golf Course. _____

12. How many (boy) sing in the glee club? _____

13. The restaurant roasted five (turkey) for Thanksgiving dinner. _____

14. All the hotel's (key) are in use. _____

15. During our vacation in Banff we saw three (play). _____

16. There are six (day) until we sail for home. _____

17. One of my favorite (city) is Vancouver. _____

18. One of his many (folly) is dressing in outlandish clothes. _____

19. The waiters' (tray) were heaped high with food. _____

20. The (cry) of the baby were heard outside the window. _____

21. The (monkey) in the zoo like to show off for visitors. _____

22. The (ray) of the sun almost blinded us. _____

23. There are many (way) to cook hamburger on a barbecue.

_____

24. How many different kinds of (clay) are there? _____

25. That prison has twelve (turnkey). _____

Nouns Ending in *o*

The plural of nouns ending in *o*, preceded by a vowel, is formed by adding *s*.

cameo—cameos   folio—folios   studio—studios   Eskimo—Eskimos

The plural of most nouns ending in *o*, preceded by a consonant, is formed by adding *s*, but for some nouns of this class the plural is formed by adding *es*.

piano—pianos   tomato—tomatoes
soprano—sopranos   potato—potatoes
auto—autos   echo—echoes
solo—solos   hero—heroes

Some words, such as *motto*, *mango*, and *mosquito*, may end with either *s* or *es* in their plural form. The safest thing to do is to memorize the few words that always add *es*, and then consult a dictionary when in doubt about others.

Spelling Plurals Correctly. In each sentence below, change the singular noun given in parentheses into the plural form. Write it in the blank after the sentence. Consult a dictionary when in doubt.

Example: The (potato) are especially good this year. *potatoes*

1. The art of the (Eskimo) is famous throughout the world. _____

2. I had my mother's (cameo) set in a ring and a necklace. _____

3. We were all listening to our (radio) at nine o'clock. _____

4. How can our little living room hold two (piano)? _____

5. Uncle Joe was given a welcome usually reserved for (hero). _____

6. The artists work in their (studio) each morning. _____

7. Thousands of (auto) in town have created a traffic jam. _____

8. We all had steaks and baked (potato) for dinner. _____

9. Helen Brent and Lois Walls will each sing two (solo) in the concert.

_____

10. How many (soprano) sing in the girls' glee club? _____

11. Mrs. Hopkins is going to can the (tomato) from her garden. _____

12. That cowboy has ridden in (rodeo) all over the West. _____

13. There are eight (alto) in the chorus. _____

14. The two men accompanied the singers on their (banjo). _____

15. How much fodder is stored in those (silo)? _____

16. (Folio) are very large books. _____

17. We work in our (studio) every afternoon. _____

18. We heard the (echo) from far away. _____

19. Our two (radio) are in the repair shop. _____

20. Barb and Nancy accompanied us on their two (piano). _____

Plural of Nouns Ending in *f* or *ff*

The plural of most nouns ending in *f* or *ff* is formed regularly by adding *s*.

 chiefs staffs gulfs sheriffs

The plural of some nouns ending in *f* or *fe* is formed by changing the *f* or *fe* to *ve* and adding *-s*.

 wife—wives wolf—wolves leaf—leaves
 thief—thieves life—lives loaf—loaves
 elf—elves calf—calves half—halves

Spelling Plurals Correctly. In each of the following sentences, change the singular noun given in parentheses into the plural form. Write it in the blank after the sentence.

 Example: All the regional police (chief) attended the conference. *chiefs*

1. The autumn (leaf) are scattering over the countryside. _____

2. Santa Claus and his (elf) are portrayed in the store's windows every Christmas. _____

3. The snow completely covered the (roof) of our houses. _____

4. How many (loaf) of bread should I buy? _____

5. The (life) of famous scientists make fascinating reading. _____

6. The (staff) of nutrition institutes from all over the nation are meeting in Guelph. _____

7. How many (gulf) can you name in the eastern hemisphere? _____

8. (Thief) emptied the house of its valuable paintings. _____

9. Have you worked out the (proof) for the geometry problems? _____

10. Have you read much about the life of the Prime Ministers? _____

11. The (wife) of the cabinet members will attend the swearing-in ceremony. _____

12. The Indian wolf and the Japanese wolf are the most common kinds of Asian (wolf). _____

13. The fire (chief) of all the regions are meeting in the city. _____

14. The little (waif) begged for money on the streets of Bombay. _____

15. Place the (knife) on the right of the plate. _____

16. Do you know the song called "Bringing in the (Sheaf)?" _____

17. The farmer has eight new (calf) this spring. _____

18. A good summer salad is made by filling the (half) of a cantaloupe with chicken salad. _____

19. What are your political (belief)? _____

20. You can make the table longer by putting in extra (leaf). _____

Nouns with Irregular Plurals

The plural of some nouns is formed by a change of spelling.

tooth—teeth	crisis—crises
foot—feet	basis—bases
man—men	goose—geese
woman—women	mouse—mice
child—children	phenomenon—phenomena
ox—oxen	datum—data
hypothesis—hypotheses	index—indexes

The plural and singular forms are the same for a few nouns.

sheep	Chinese
deer	Portuguese
cattle	corps

Spelling Plurals Correctly. Read each of the sentences below. Where necessary, change the singular noun given in parentheses into the plural form. Write the correct plural form in the blank after the sentence. If the plural form is spelled the same as the singular form already used, place a **C** in the blank.

Example: My two (foot) are not quite the same size. ___*feet*___

1. The dentist will clean my (tooth) tomorrow. _____
2. The (Portuguese) were great explorers in the fifteenth century. _____
3. We saw the (mouse) scampering about in their cages. _____
4. Tell me all the (basis) for your decision. _____
5. How many divisions do those two (corps) comprise? _____
6. Twelve (child) are attending the story hour at the library. _____
7. Our village has hired two new (policewoman). _____
8. Mr. Grady has large herds of (cattle) on his two farms. _____
9. How many (Chinese) have come to Canada to live? _____
10. The (woman) are holding a rummage sale this week. _____
11. (Ox) are still used to pull carts in some parts of Spain. _____
12. It took four (man) to move that huge marble-topped table into the house. _____
13. We saw three (deer) on the island last week. _____
14. What do you think are the three most fascinating natural (phenomenon)? _____
15. The (man) in the orchestra wore tuxedos for their concert. _____
16. We searched through the (index) of both books. _____
17. We saw a flock of Canada (goose) overhead. _____
18. I think that this is just one of life's many (crisis)! _____
19. In Australia, the stockman on a (sheep) station looks after the (sheep). _____
20. Let's start with two (hypothesis). _____

Names and Compound Nouns   173

The plural of a name is formed by adding *s* or *es*.

William Martin—the Martins   Michael Corey—the Coreys
Bruce Means—the Meanses   Jack Voss—the Vosses

The Plural of Compound Nouns. When a compound noun is written without a hyphen, the plural is formed at the end of the word.

handful—handfuls   doghouse—doghouses   cupful—cupfuls

When a compound noun is made up of a noun plus a modifier, the plural is added to the noun.

brothers-in-law (*in-law* is a modifier.)
attorneys-general (*general* is a modifier.)
notaries public (*public* is a modifier.)

EXCEPTIONS   drive-ins, stand-bys, lean-tos, fill-ins

Spelling Plurals Correctly. In each of the following sentences, change the singular noun given in parentheses into the plural form. Write the correct plural form of the noun in the blank after the sentence. Watch for modifiers.

1. I drank two (glassful) of water. _____
2. How many (sister-in-law) does Barbara have? _____
3. There is a meeting of our town's (notary public) at ten o'clock. _____
4. The (Morse) live next door to us. _____
5. The little girl gave me a basket filled with five (handful) of dandelions.

_____

6. We have three (doghouse) in our back yard. _____
7. How many (Governor General) have we had since 1867? _____
8. The (Storms), our next-door neighbors, are on vacation. _____
9. Both of my (brother-in-law) are bankers. _____
10. The (Sheardown) attended the conference to learn more about music administration. _____
11. How many (attorney-general) served between 1960 and 1970? _____
12. There are four (drive-in) on this street. _____
13. (Lean-to) were added to the structure to house the gardening equipment. _____
14. The (Evans) are playing golf with the Millers. _____
15. Which (right-of-way) does the railroad occupy? _____
16. (Justice of the peace) have often married couples. _____
17. He drank two (cupful) of tea. _____
18. The (chief of police) from all over our county are meeting today. _____
19. Several (hanger-on) waited outside the hotel. _____
20. My three (brother-in-law) all have new cars. _____

Review: The Plurals of Nouns 174

Spelling Plurals Correctly. In each of the following sentences, change the singular noun given in parentheses into the plural form. Write it in the blank after the sentence.

Example: The waiter dropped all of the (dish) on his tray. *dishes*

1. My cousins and I attend different (church). _____
2. Grover had trouble moving the (box) off the steps. _____
3. Our teacher gives (test) every Friday. _____
4. The quarterback threw three touchdown (pass). _____
5. It is the peak of the season for (cherry). _____
6. Each of the team's (play) was second-guessed by the opponents. _____
7. The engaged couple attended (party) every night for a week. _____
8. I ordered two French (pastry) for dessert. _____
9. The artists' (studio) were in the attic. _____
10. The movers were upset to see two grand (piano). _____
11. Mom put (tomato) in the salad. _____
12. The (hero) were awarded their medals at the ceremony. _____
13. Beverly Sills and Leontyne Price are famous (soprano). _____
14. How many (wife) did Henry the VIII have? _____
15. The Indian (chief) were in full tribal dress. _____
16. The (knife) and forks were all spotted. _____
17. These (shelf) need dusting. _____
18. My (foot) swell in the hot weather. _____
19. Have you had your wisdom (tooth) pulled? _____
20. All of the (child) were dismissed early. _____
21. The (ox) were pulling the heavy load easily. _____
22. We added two (teaspoonful) of vanilla to the batter. _____
23. The (commander-in-chief) from the warring nations met. _____
24. Both (house) have been painted white. _____
25. How many (brother-in-law) do you have? _____

Numbers in Writing

Numbers that can be expressed in fewer than four words are usually spelled out; longer numbers are written in figures.

> Tickets for the play cost *three* dollars.
> That actress has *thirty-seven* pairs of shoes!
> Our house-to-house drive collected $1879.00

A number beginning a sentence is spelled out.

> Three hundred students attended the assembly.

Figures in Writing. Figures are used to express dates, street and room numbers, telephone numbers, page numbers, decimals, degrees, and percentages.

> In April, 1975, our address was 645 Prospect Avenue.
> The class in room 318 is at work on algebra problems.
> Only 60 percent of the students attended the debate.

Writing Numbers Correctly. Most of the following sentences contain an error in the writing of a number or figure. Underline the error and rewrite it correctly in the blank after the sentence. Three sentences are correct and need no revisions.

1. Thirty-seven people replied to the ad. _____
2. Mr. Bruce's estate amounted to $500 000.00 _____
3. Connie's room number is two hundred twenty-nine. _____
4. Where did you live in December, nineteen hundred eighty? _____
5. 4 people were injured in the accident. _____
6. Mrs. Miller wrote a check for two thousand four hundred sixty-seven dollars. _____
7. The exhibit was held on July twenty-seventh, nineteen hundred.

_____

8. The temperature in the room was thirty-five degrees Celsius! _____
9. More than three hundred people attended the auction. _____
10. Admission will be $3.00 for each student. _____
11. Work the problems on page thirty-one for tomorrow. _____
12. I'm sure that eighty percent of the teachers believe as we do. _____
13. The women of the church made $2236.00 on their bazaar. _____
14. The selling price of the house was eighty-eight thousand, three hundred dollars. _____
15. 650 tickets were printed. _____
16. Of the students at Brampton High, sixty percent are studying a foreign language. _____
17. We bought our car in nineteen hundred eighty-one. _____
18. Don's temperature was forty degrees Celsius. _____
19. Our club earned 84 dollars at its bake sale. _____
20. For tomorrow, please read the poem on page twenty-one. _____

Abbreviations in Writing

Abbreviations may be used for most titles that come before and after proper names, for names of government agencies, and in dates.

BEFORE PROPER NAMES   Dr., Mr., Mrs., Ms., Rev., Capt., Hon.,

AFTER PROPER NAMES   Jr., Sr., D. D. S., Ph. D.

DATES AND TIMES   P. M., B. C.

GOVERNMENT AGENCIES   PSC, TRB, CMHC, (there are no periods after government agency abbreviations)

The titles *Honorable* and *Reverend* are not abbreviated when preceded by *the*.

In ordinary writing, abbreviations are not acceptable for names of countries and states, months and days of the week, nor words that are part of addresses or firm names.

UNACCEPTABLE	BETTER
We went to B.C.	We went to British Columbia
The date was Tues., Dec. 5.	The date was Tuesday, December 5.
Bell Can. sent a bill.	Bell Canada sent a bill.

In ordinary writing, do not abbreviate words standing for measurements, names of school courses, *Christmas*, *page*, and *chapter*.

Correcting Errors in Abbreviations. Underline the errors in the abbreviations in the following sentences. Correct each error in the blank after the sentence.

1. Al will start work for Connaught Laboratories in Oct. _____

2. Mary is the sec. of our French club. _____

3. Cap. Sims has had years of experience on ships. _____

4. I am registered for Engl. 101 next fall. _____

5. Our train was 15 min. late. _____

6. The Blacks are moving to N.S. _____

7. Have you had a raise in the last yr? _____

8. Can. looked good to me when I returned from Europe. _____

_____

9. The Rev. Harvey Jensen will preach the sermon. _____

10. Bob works for the Hopkins Mfg. Co. _____

11. Where will you spend Xmas this year? _____

12. Our P.M. is one of the most important people in Canada.

_____

13. I've been to the West Coast, but I've never been to P.E.I. _____

_____

14. Bill Clark is the treas. of our class. _____

15. The Min. of Foreign Affairs often represents our nation abroad.

_____

The Use of Italics   177

The word *italics* is a printer's term. It refers to a kind of type. When a writer wants the printer to set a word in italic type, he or she underlines it in the manuscript.

Titles of complete books and plays, of newspapers, magazines, works of art, and long musical compositions are printed in italics. The names of ships, trains, and airplanes are also printed in italics.

> His poetry has appeared in *The Saturday Review*
> *Newsweek* helps me keep up with the news.
> *My Fair Lady* is based on Shaw's *Pygmalion*.

Foreign words that are widely used, such as *entrepreneur* and *chauffeur*, are printed in regular type. Words and phrases that have not become naturalized in our language are printed in italics: *cum laude, bon vivant*.

Italics are used for words, letters, or figures referred to as such.

> There are too many *and's* in your first sentence.

Italics (underlining) are used to give special emphasis to words or phrases. Use italics for emphasis only to make the meaning clear.

> I've *always* admired him.
> Did you say you owe *me* some money?

Using Italics Correctly. In each of the following sentences, underline the words that should be placed in italics.

> Example: Jim graduated <u>cum laude</u> from the university.

1. Dan saw the statue called the Little Mermaid in Denmark.
2. After reading a review of The Freedom Seekers, I wanted to read the book.
3. My brother was graduated magna cum laude from the University of Regina.
4. Do you prefer Maclean's or Newsweek to keep you informed?
5. In 1971 we travelled from Liverpool to Canada on the Queen Elizabeth II.
6. Don't write censer when you mean censor.
7. You have three if's in your last sentence.
8. In England the word laboratory is accented on the second syllable.
9. Did you ever see the musical Oklahoma?
10. Mr. Swenson has read the Toronto Star for forty years.
11. Have you ever tried any of the recipes in Gourmet magazine?
12. What we call a hardware store is called the ironmonger's in Great Britain.
13. The there should have been written their.
14. We all enjoyed seeing Anne of Green Gables on the stage.
15. Someone who loves good living is called a bon vivant.

Review: Good Manuscript Form

Writing Numbers Correctly. The following sentences contain errors in the writing of numbers or figures. Underlne each error and rewrite it correctly on the blank after the sentence.

Example: Ray was born in <u>nineteen forty-four</u>. *1944*

1. Only three hundred people attended—less than fifty percent. _____

2. Bob earns 3 dollars an hour for mowing lawns. _____

3. The assignment is to read up to page seventy. _____

4. It took 6 hours to free the trapped miner. _____

5. Dad's tax bill was one thousand, three hundred sixty two dollars, and fifty cents. _____

6. The attendance at the game was about 5 000. _____

7. The temperature dropped to seventeen degrees below zero. _____

8. Our classroom number is two twenty-two. _____

9. My baby brother was born on October third. _____

10. Admission is $3.50 for students. _____

Correcting Errors in Abbreviations. Underline the error in abbreviation in each of the following sentences. Correct the error on the blank after each sentence.

Example: Each class in our school is fifty <u>min.</u> long. *minutes*

1. The Rev. James Bell is addressing the congregation. _____

2. Your next appointment is Tues. afternoon. _____

3. Hostess Food Products Ltd. make delicious pastries. _____

4. We hope to spend the winter in Calif. _____

5. The planeload of refugees arrived in Tor. _____

Using Italics Correctly. In each of the following sentences, underline the words that should be placed in italics.

Example: Are <u>you</u> telling <u>me</u> what to do?

1. The latest issue of Maclean's has an interesting feature article.

2. Susan graduated summa cum laude from Dalhousie University.

3. The adding machine misprinted all of the seven's.

4. The Titanic's sinking was a shock to nautical engineers.

5. We are looking forward to reading Macbeth in English class.